2250
99135

CULTURE AND LANGUAGE

The Black American Experience

CULTURE AND LANGUAGE

The Black American Experience

William S. Hall
THE ROCKEFELLER UNIVERSITY

Roy O. Freedle
EDUCATIONAL TESTING SERVICE

Hemisphere Publishing Corporation
Washington, D.C.

A HALSTED PRESS BOOK

John Wiley & Sons
New York   London   Sydney   Toronto

Hemisphere Publishing Corporation
1025 Vermont Avenue, N.W., Washington, D.C. 20005

Distributed solely by Halsted Press, a Division of
John Wiley & Sons, Inc., New York.

Library of Congress Cataloging in Publication Data

Hall, William S.
    Culture and language

    Includes bibliographical references and index.
    1. Language and culture. 2. Negroes—Language. 3. English language in the United States—Dialects. 4. Negroes—Psychology. 5. Educational tests and measurements—United States. 6. Social science research—United States. I. Freedle, Roy O., joint author. II. Title.
P35.H3   301.2'1   75-12534
0-470-34156-4

Printed in the United States of America

To the late Professor Lorenzo Dow Turner

CONTENTS

PREFACE

This book reviews the various ways in which the black experience in the United States has been treated in social science. It points out a dilemma that ensues from the absence of a true ethnography of the black experience in the United States. This absence has made it difficult to assess such matters as the cognitive basis of reading and dialect systems, particularly as these relate to the black experience. We criticize the melting pot myth, which asserts that all Americans share an identical culture and are equal in it. If this myth were taken seriously, black Americans who find themselves disproportionately represented among the poor, the uneducated, and the unemployed would have to place the blame for their current condition on themselves. While some might take this view seriously, we regard it as absurd.

We maintain that old cultural patterns persist over many generations, in spite of a drive toward homogeneity. Such cultural differences form a coherent organized pattern; and these patterns have consequences for preferred modes of interaction, communication, problem solving, and self-identity or self-concept. Because these patterns, which persist over time, are themselves interacting with other group patterns that have different origins, tensions develop. One group may win momentary political and economic advantage over the other; and such momentary circumstances may become confounded with the ethnic origins of the people. This confounding has real psychological consequences that can not be explained by such superficial devices as gene pool differences. But, while psychological, the problem can have disastrous consequences for those who must endure day-by-day oppression.

This book discusses the dynamics of these cultural and cognitive forces and seeks to offer some suggestions for bringing about circumstances that may actually accelerate the movement toward a true melting pot.

This book will be of interest to a wide audience of professionals in the fields of psychology, sociology, education, and linguistics. It also is addressed to students at both the graduate and undergraduate levels of language teaching, language development, language learning in monocultural and bicultural settings, and standard and nonstandard language.

We wish to acknowledge the critical comments of Dalton Jones, Raymond P. McDermott, Klaus Riegel, and Stephen Wright for their many suggestions which greatly improved the manuscript. A special note of thanks is due Jack Maisel for his fine editing of the manuscript.

William S. Hall
Roy O. Freedle

ILLUSTRATIONS

TABLES

1

INTRODUCTION

Although our book focuses primarily on black American language, to interpret language comprehensively we must include in our conception of it the larger social sphere in which it resides. Inasmuch as any language can be said to reflect a culture, discussion of it must be addressed to the larger whole of which it is a part; for black American language, then, the relevant aspects of the larger culture in which black culture functions as a salient subset as well as particular features of the subculture must both be taken into account. This is necessary because black Americans interact not only with one another but also with other Americans.

In analyzing the larger social sphere, we find a variety of factors that are pertinent to such an analysis. One's self-concept, for example, can play a critical part in the types of roles one may play in communication. If one's self-concept is negative, such a view will manifest itself by perhaps altering the way one speaks in social discourse.

In addition to self-concept, we must consider the interactive cause-effect relationships which have the characteristics of feedback loops. In examining the feedback loops, we will perforce note a critical distinction between wholistic and embedded subcultures, treating the black American culture as one embedded within the larger wholistic American culture. The thrust of our argument will be that a subculture, particularly one that is primarily separate and unequal, will give rise to certain characteristic behaviors among its members. One such behavior is that of a unique system of language. Owing to its uniqueness, this system of language will have consequences for the user that may have impact on his self-concept as well as on his cognitive performance.

Even though key concepts such as *registers*, *self-concept*, *feedback loops*, and *wholistic versus embedded cultures* are available to us, we are at the mere beginning of the empirical work that fleshes out these concepts. Therefore, this book will also attempt to define the stage on which these concepts interact and to proffer suggestions about how future investigative work may proceed.

Traditionally, ethnographic psychology has focused on large units of cultural differences among wholistic, self-sufficient cultures. In crosscultural comparisons little specific attention has been given to cultures embedded within a prevailing culture. We distinguish here between *encapsulated* and *embedded* since much work has been done on encapsulated cultures (for example, American Indians) but little has been done on embedded cultures (for example, American blacks). The embedded subculture is one that must function as if it were an integral part of the larger culture with few of the rights and privileges of that larger culture; the encapsulated subculture is allowed to maintain its cultural practices in such a way that their impact on those of the prevailing culture is minimal or nonexistent. Unlike larger cultures, subcultures are not totally self-sufficient; nor are they independent. Moreover, subcultures typically have little political power, are usually economically oppressed by the dominant culture, and are viewed, we believe, with suspicion and often treated with malice by the major culture. The unique position of being in a subculture that is encompassed by another more paramount culture causes a person to have many characteristic ways of behaving that tend to set him or her apart; being set apart, in turn, often serves as an invitation for further oppression and discrimination.

This book will develop the theoretical position that the cognitive functioning, the language used, and the self-concept of oppressed minority groups can be best understood through ethnographic enlightenment. The ethnographic approach applied to subcultures clarifies and makes evident the ecological relations which shape the day-to-day behaviors of their members. Our main thesis is that the problem of group differences (in such matters as cognitive functioning, for example) does not stem primarily from gene-pool, IQ, racial-group membership, or language differences, as has been suggested of late, but rather from a particular set of social forces (e.g., inequitable economic situations, political power of one group over another, etc.) that operate over time to produce certain psychological results in groups that may make them appear to be pathological or deviant in certain situations.[1]

In this respect, wholistic cultures have escaped somewhat such pejorative conditions, largely as a result of geographic separation and some degree of economic self-sufficiency. But

[1] This is not to suggest that there are not some physical characteristics that occasionally mark an individual as black, white, or oriental (Gottesman, 1968; Levine, 1970); nor that individuals do not differ in terms of intelligence or language (Ferguson, 1973; Halliday, 1973; Labov, 1970). Certainly such differences can always be found, but they are of limited explanatory use by themselves (Anastasi, 1958). While they may work for certain everyday uses, in the long run, they are theoretically flawed distinctions.

minority groups in embedded subcultures must always bear
the burden of these social forces. They are thus, in this
special way, different from members of wholistic cultures.

Clearly, some of the cultures studied by ethnographic
psychologists fall between subcultures and more wholistic
ones. We have mentioned that some subcultures can be
distinguished as encapsulated versus embedded. One might
also suggest additional categories so as to classify, for
example, the Commonwealth nations under Great Britain. To
be sure, these additional categories suggest an intriguing
theoretical problem, but our purpose here is not to dwell on
these many possible distinctions, but rather to take, as given,
the legitimacy of the distinction between embedded and
wholistic cultures and to explore this concept for its
clarification of the black American experience.

It will be useful to now summarize some of the work in
general ethnographic psychology so as to have ready
reference to the findings that apply to differences among
wholistic cultures that are in some respect politically and
socially free.

II

SOME GENERALIZATIONS
ABOUT WHOLISTIC CULTURES
AND SUBCULTURES

WHOLISTIC CULTURES

Traditionally, crosscultural studies of wholistic cultures have focused on the concept of race as the chief source for explaining differences. The recent literature (see, for example, Boas, 1905; Downs and Bleibtreu, 1969; Kroeber, 1948; and Montagu, 1964, 1965) indicates, however, that in anthropology, the concept of race is not an adequate explanation of cultural differences because the concept as we know it has an elusive referent.

According to Alland (1973) and Downs (1971), physical anthropologists who specialize in the study of race and its definitions have as yet been unable to agree upon an adequate system for classifying people according to race; hence, they are unable to state with any degree of scientific certainty the number of races that exist. Various schemata advanced over the years have ranged from a tripartite classification (Caucasoid, Mongoloid, and Negroid) system up through a system employing 300 divisions. The uncertainty of these schemata stems from their inability to draw arbitrary lines of demarcation on essentially continuous distributions of traits. For example, on the feature skin color, it is impossible to justify any one point of demarcation between light-skin and dark skin. The same problem arises for such other human features as the curliness of hair, profuseness of body hair, arm-body ratio, and prognathism. Downs contends that if the concept of race is unclear, it is fruitless to attempt to employ race differences in accounting for behavioral differences. One may note that the behavioral differences of concern to Downs and Alland were primarily those associated with culture. The identical problem exists when one focuses upon presumptive causal· analyses in explaining black and white behavioral differences in America.

When we concentrate on seeking to understand the cognitive functioning of minorities in America, their language and cognitive processing differences (if any) are attributable not to race but more appropriately to sociohistorical events (see, for example, Alland, 1973; Cole and Scribner, 1974; Frake, 1964; Harris, 1968; Herskovits, 1965).

The underlying assumption in research on ethnographic psychology is that there are cultural differences, but these differences do not negate universals. The principle is most aptly expressed by the statement that cultural differences in thought are owing not to process differences but to content ones. The view has analogs in the fields of both linguistics and psychology. Chomsky (1968) hypothesized that any human language generates a potentially infinite number of well formed sentences from a finite set of rules. The assumption here is that all languages around the world are equivalent with respect to generative capacity, even though the particular content of the rules may differ among them. The psychology analog is perhaps best summarized in the work of Piaget (1966). He views the development of intellectual growth as a succession of logical structures such that at each stage the individual aspects of mental life reflect the internal structuring of that stage. The stages and their succession in time are considered universal. The effect of culture is that of accelerating or retarding the time at which each stage is entered. It can be said, consequently, that both Piaget and Chomsky posit universal characteristics of cognition.

But universals need not negate differences (see, for example, Geertz, 1970). A somewhat contrasting viewpoint with respect to Chomsky and Piaget is provided by the work of Luria (1971) and Vygotsky (1962), inasmuch as their approach stresses ways to account for both differences and similarities across cultures. Vygotsky maintains that process as well as content changes can occur in cultural groups over time. He postulates that the invariant aspects upon which process changes are built have to do with such elementary forms as sensory activation, movement, attention, and short-term memory. From these elementary forms evolve the more complex functions such as voluntary memory, directive attention, voluntary movement, and abstract thought. These complex processes are then further organized into functional systems, which are subject to historical changes as new practical and theoretical activities are engaged in by the culture.

Part and parcel of traditional crosscultural comparisons is the charting of relationships between culture and language. The best-known hypothesis dealing with the interaction of language and culture is the Whorfian hypothesis (see Whorf, 1956), which contends that the language we use affects the way we perceive the world; that is, language seems to shape or place limits on our thoughts. The following propositions underlie this view:

1. *linguistic relativity*, which maintains that individuals who speak different languages experience the world differently
2. *linguistic determinism*, which postulates a causal directionality from language to cognitive processes

A review of the current literature reflects an emphasis on linguistic relativity. Several levels of language—lexicon and grammar—have been investigated with respect to Whorf's hypothesis. With respect to the lexicon, Hockett (1954) concludes that languages differ not in terms of what can be said but rather in terms of the relative ease with which some specific thought can be expressed. Thus, he contends, even if a particular language does not have a word for an intended concept, the language is flexible enough that other means can be found to express the concept. A study by Carroll and Casagrande (1958), for example, suggests that verb types do influence the linguistic groupings that people make.

With respect to linguistic determinism, the literature on the relationship between culture and language actually reflects efforts to investigate linguistic universality in terms of connotative meaning (the Whorfian hypothesis deals mainly with referential aspects of language). Several studies using the semantic differential attest to the existence of three factors underlying the connotative aspects of the lexicon across most of the languages of the world: good–bad, strong–weak, and fast–slow, which are evaluative, potency, and activity factors respectively. In addition, verbal-visual synesthesia, that is, the connection between a word (for example, *happy*) and a pictorial representation (for example, an arrow pointing upward) has been found to have cross-cultural generality. Also languages appear to share levels of construction such as phonology (sound systems), grammar, and lexicon.

THE SUBCULTURAL EXPERIENCE

In trying to list generalizations that apply to the subcultural experience in America we are greatly hampered by a history of ethnocentrism in some aspects of social science research. Many of the generalizations (e.g., intelligence differences) that have been applied to embedded populations are in our view incorrect, in that one can demonstrate that they stem from an ethnocentric position. It may be useful at this point to delineate the nature of this ethnocentrism before presenting a more ethnographically based review of the subcultural experience of black Americans.

Many outsiders surveying the black American subculture are apt to label as pathological many of the behavior patterns that they observe. This is so because early portrayals of the black American have been largely in terms of a cultural deficit model. While this model implies the concept of an embedded subculture within a prevailing culture, it fails to capture the essential feature of one culture's being subordinated to another, as we have mentioned earlier. It is true that there may be a cultural difference between the black and the white American, but what one must not lose sight of is that historically this difference is augmented by the separation and inequality of these two groups.

An additional concept that has been used in discussing black American behavior patterns is *cultural pluralism*. However useful the concept is as it stands, it can be further clarified by noting its relationship to our contrast between a wholistic culture and embedded subcultures. It thereby suggests to our minds that the different systems of values and behavior prevalent in various cultures cannot necessarily be placed on an evaluative scale wherein those of one are deemed better than the other. Later we will make frequent references to the traditional approaches taken in characterizing the black American experience in terms of cultural deficit, cultural difference, and cultural pluralism. When necessary, we will reinterpret these labels to clarify the argument with respect to the major principle of wholistic versus embedded and subordinated subcultures.

Use of the cultural deficit model as the springboard to explain behavior patterns has a long history in social science research. We assert that its starting point is *ethnocentrism* and the position that emanates from it is *ethnocentric*. A working characterization of this position with regard to black Americans can be found in the recent writings of Baratz and Baratz (1970) and McDermott (1974). Baratz and Baratz state that "the absence of a meaningful conception of Negro culture has forced the interpretation of almost all psychology's data on the Negro into two seemingly dichotomous categories—either that of biological incapacity (genetic inferiority) or social deviance and pathology (environmental deprivation)." McDermott (1974) notes that "ethnocentric behavior is a product of more than just confusion. As a self-fulfilling prophecy, it helps to make the world what it must be in order for ethnocentrism to be maintained even by 'scientific analysis.' "

Such a position raises the question of why social science has failed to integrate relevant elements of black cultural life into its research. Drawing on the work of Baratz and Baratz, we propose the following four reasons:

1. the normativistic nature of the fundamental model
2. the sociopolitical myths surrounding social scientists' conception of subcultural assimilation into the majority culture
3. the error concerning the fundamental notion of culture

4. the confusion of the black middle class and the white liberal about the nature of culturally rooted behavioral differences

The normative model sets up criteria of behavior against which individuals and groups are measured. The ethnocentrism here is that the social scientist often attempts to assess behavior by using criteria assumed to be universal when they may be in fact idiosyncratic to one group.

Baratz and Baratz (1970) discuss three American sociopolitical myths that have contributed to the denial of cultural differences between American blacks and the majority culture. The first of these is the melting pot myth, and its corollary, egalitarianism. Briefly, the myth holds that America is the melting pot society in which peoples from diverse cultures have come together and have created an American culture distinct from the individual cultures that contributed to it. Moreover, this American society is said to be the result of the best elements of these diverse cultures. But according to the Baratzes, the melting pot idea has aided and abetted the misinterpretation of the substance of the basic doctrine of egalitarianism, subverting it from "all men are created equal" to "all men are created equal if they behave in the same manner."

The second myth that the Baratzes discuss is the interpretation of certain behaviors peculiar to blacks as evidence of genetic inferiority—for example, habits of dress, patterns of dialect, and the type of extended family kinship system.

The third and final myth has been labeled the "myth of the Negro past," after Herskovits (1941). This myth asserts that certain notions of social scientists concerning the processes of acculturation have led to the assumption that blacks have lost all their characteristic African behaviors merely because they left Africa and lived in the United States for generations in slavery. The erroneous analysis of the functioning of the black past has contributed to social scientists' misinformation concerning the significance of historical roots. Indeed, Glazer and Moynihan (1963) have stated that "the Negro is only an American and nothing else. He has no values and culture to guard and protect. ..." Baratz and Baratz (1970) maintain, however, that implicit in such statements is a lack of understanding of the acculturative process. They note:

> ... it was assumed that, for example, since Afro-Americans no longer spoke African languages, no longer wore African dress, that they therefore retained no cultural distinctiveness. This assumption left the social scientists with no other alternative than to wrongly describe the creolized Negro dialect used by the Afro-American as poorly learned English, the matrifocal family unit so prevalent in the lower class Negro society as "evidence of male emasculation," the extended kinship systems as "disorganized families," and the clothing choices as "poor taste."

They further point out that

> Perhaps the best example of how existing cultural patterns effect the adaptation of new forms is in examining how the Afro-American culture in the United States has dealt with efforts to infuse African styles into the creolized culture. The "black is beautiful" emphasis in black rhetoric has not simply transferred African hairstyles to the Negro-American community, but rather has modified them in accordance with certain distinctively New World Afro-American cultural values; namely, that the female should have longer hair than the male. Thus, one finds the adaptation of the African bush by Afro-American girls but with the Americanized aspect of having large "long hair" bushes as opposed to the typical close-cut bush of African women. Again we find that Afro-American women, rather than taking up the dressing styles of

African women, have instead modified the African male costume—the dashiki—to suit American female dressing patterns.

The issue here seems to revolve around the social scientists' notion of cultural difference. Some (e.g., psychologists) have traditionally viewed difference in terms of a universalistic norm falsely abstracted from white middle-class culture. Others (e.g., anthropologists), abstracting from wholistic cultures, view cultural difference as an indication of the various ways different people have chosen to define their world. In our view, the anthropologists have characterized cultural difference more accurately.

Misinterpretation about the true meaning of culture and failure to recognize the cultural component involved have been sources of embarrassment to the black middle class and the white liberal in their attempts to deal with behavioral differences of subcultures. Underlying this error is a fear that discussions about differences would be used maliciously by racists to support their theories of black inferiority. Although the fear is in many instances understandable, we feel the premises from which it emanates are untenable. Real differences in cultures should be seen as strengths rather than weaknesses.

An ethnocentric posture, then, has influenced social science research in the absence of a meaningful conception of black American culture. Consequently, almost all social science data on black Americans have been interpreted as supporting either genetic inferiority or social deviance and pathology. Social science has neglected to integrate relevant elements of black culture into its research because of restrictive normative standards, melting pot myths, erroneous notions about culture, and confusion and hesitancy in discussions by the black middle class and the white liberal about culturally rooted behavior differences.

An Example of Ethnocentrism
in Social Science Research

Examples of ethnocentrism in social science are legion. An excellent illustration is the Moynihan (1965) report on the black family, particularly with Hill's (1972) study presenting a different point of view now at hand.

In the mid-sixties, Daniel P. Moynihan issued a report on the black family, which caused much furor. Moynihan's starting point in this report is the assertion that

> At the heart of the deterioration of the fabric of Negro society is the deterioration of the Negro family. . . . The role of the family in shaping character and ability is so pervasive as to be easily overlooked. The family is the basic social unit of American life; it is the basic socializing unit. By and large, adult conduct in society is learned as a child. (p. 51)

Since the family is viewed by Moynihan as centrally important to American life, he asserts that a segment of the black community is in difficulty in this regard:

> . . . the family structure of lower class Negroes is highly unstable, and in many urban centers is approaching complete breakdown . . . the emergence and increasing visibility of a Negro middle class may beguile the nation into supposing that the circumstances of the remainder of the Negro community are equally prosperous, whereas just the opposite is true at present, and is likely to continue so. (p. 51)

To buttress his position, Moynihan draws on data from the U.S. Census, the Department of Commerce, and the Bureau of Labor. Specifically, he attends to illegitimacy rates, divorce statistics, females as heads of households, and welfare dependency. When speaking of desertion, Moynihan notes that approximately 25 percent of Negro women who live in cities and have been married are now divorced, separated, or living apart from their husbands. In large cities the proportion of absent husbands is even higher; in New York City in 1960 it was 30.2 percent, not including divorces. And the number of illegitimate children per 1,000 live births increased by 11 percent among whites in the period 1940-1963, but by 68 percent among nonwhites.[1]

He likewise paints a rather grim picture of the black family through the data on divorce rates. He notes that between 1940 and 1964 there was a general increase but a far greater increase for nonwhites than for whites (40 percent and 3.6 percent, respectively). The percentage of nonwhite families headed by a female is more than double the percentage for whites. In addition, he notes that it has been estimated that by the age of 18, only a minority of black children have lived with both parents.

Finally, as crowning "evidence" of the deterioration of the black family, Moynihan discusses the extent of welfare dependency. He states that the majority of black children receive public assistance under the Assistance to Families of Dependent Children program (AFDC) at one point or another during their childhood.

The breakdown of the black family is explained by Moynihan as having its genesis in several historical processes:

1. slavery
2. reconstruction

[1] We suspect that Moynihan's data are highly unreliable, especially with regard to these facts. One is reminded of a Burundi proverb, "A man who tells no lies cannot feed his children." It is unlikely that these statistics reflect the real state of affairs, given eligibility requirements of such programs as Assistance to Families of Dependent Children (AFDC). The proportion of absent husbands is certain to be much lower than the statistics show, which would help to explain the dramatic increase in "illegitimate" births among nonwhites. However, the main point here is not the reliability of Moynihan's data, but his interpretation of them.

3. urbanization
4. unemployment
5. the wage system
6. rapid population growth

According to Moynihan, servitude in the United States differed from that elsewhere in that attitudes reflected in the concept of white supremacy, Protestantism, etc., held that a slave was different from his master in both degree and kind. Then, with the emancipation of the slaves, the Negro American family began to form in the United States on a wide scale. The Negro was given liberty, but not equality. It is important to note that the Negro male became the object of intense hostility, especially in the South.

With the exception of a few years during World War II and the Korean War, Negro unemployment has continued at disaster levels for 35 years. The wage system in the United States contributes to the continuance of this situation. And inasmuch as Negro families generally have the largest number of children and the lowest incomes, many Negro fathers literally cannot support their families. The Negro mother must frequently work because the father makes such a low wage, is unemployed, or is not present. Moynihan feels that this dependence on the mother's income undermines the position of the father and deprives the children of the kind of attention, particularly in school matters, that is now a standard feature of middle-class upbringing.

The major consequence of this pattern is what Moynihan calls a *tangle of pathology*. The Negro community has been forced into a matriarchical structure that, because it is so out of line with that of the rest of society, seriously retards the progress of the group as a whole and imposes a crushing burden on the Negro man and consequently on a great many Negro women as well.

How does Moynihan's report fit the criteria of ethno-centrism delineated earlier? To begin with, the author focuses on the weaknesses of the black family in terms of what white families are like, thus reflecting a single normative notion of family life. At no time does he ask what makes a black family viable. He notes, for example, that a quarter of married black women are living apart from their husbands. The fact that three quarters do not fit this category goes unnoticed. Certainly, this is the majority. He also points out that the proportion of absent husbands is higher for nonwhite than for white families (30.2 percent in New York City). Again, we point out that 69.8 percent of the husbands are present and that this is the majority. Similarly, while 56 percent of nonwhite children receive AFDC at some point in their lives, there are still 44 percent who do not, a fact that Moynihan fails to mention. Nor does he pause to wonder if the different rates of illegitimacy between blacks and whites might not reflect, in part, the societally superior position that white women have historically held in our culture, which allows them to conceal illegitimacy more easily. Moreover, Moyni-han has pursued no substantive discussion concerning the scarcity of jobs for the unskilled, who have been denied access to the means of getting jobs because of the pervasive presence of racism in our culture.

In sum, Moynihan's report reflects no meaningful concep-tion of the black family or of black life in general. Thus, his interpretation of a tangle of pathology as its overriding characteristic is fallacious and reflects the ease with which ethnocentrism in social science research evolves.

An Alternative Approach

While several alternatives to Moynihan's explanation can be found in the social science literature (see, for example,

Hill, 1972; Leacock, 1971; Valentine, 1968, 1971; and Young, 1970, 1974), we shall illustrate these alternatives from Hill's fine book. Hill gives a quite different version of the black family and takes exception to Moynihan's views. Hill notes that "the great majority of black families . . . are not characterized by criminality, delinquency, drug addiction or desertion. . . ." Hill's starting point is to look at the black family's strengths, those characteristics of the black life-style that have contributed to the survival of the black family. He defines family strength as "traits which facilitate the ability of the family to meet the needs of its members and the demands made upon it by systems outside the family unit. They are necessary for the survival and maintenance of effective family networks."

Drawing on the discussion of Otto (see Hill, 1972), who lists a number of traits contributing to family strengths and cohesion, Hill examines the literature on black families and finds five characteristics that have been functional for their survival, development, and stability:

1. strong kinship bonds
2. strong work orientation
3. adaptability of family roles
4. strong achievement orientation
5. strong religious orientation

Strong kinship bonds are reflected in several ways in the black family. For one thing, black families have traditionally absorbed minors and the elderly into their households. Recent census data reveal that black families are much more likely than are white families to take in other young relatives. In husband–wife families, 3 percent of white families compared with 13 percent of black families have taken in relatives under 18. In black families headed by a woman, there is an even greater tendency to absorb other related children: 41 percent compared with 7 percent of similarly situated white women have relatives under 18 living with them. But the families headed by elderly black women take in the highest proportion (48 percent) of children.

Moreover, a perusal of the literature reveals that extended family relationships have historically been greater among blacks than among whites. At the turn of the century, doubling up was a common occurrence in black families, particularly among new arrivals to urban areas. A system of informal adoption has served to strengthen the kinship bonds among black families. Even today, a very small percentage of illegitimate black babies, as compared with white babies, are formally adopted or placed in foster homes or institutions.

Black families can also be characterized as having a strong work orientation. The black poor in the recent past were more likely to work than were the white poor: three-fifths of the black poor worked as compared with about half of the white poor. The work ethic can be seen further in the presence of a working wife in the majority of black families: about two-thirds of the wives in black families as compared with half of the wives in white families.

Although blacks are twice as likely to be unemployed as are whites, studies of employment histories in black communities reveal a high degree of job stability among the majority of black men. Recent data (see Hill, 1972) comparing black and white male workers found that 80 percent of the blacks as opposed to 60 percent of the whites had held their current jobs for at least three years. And almost one-half of the blacks as contrasted with only one-third of the whites had held their jobs for ten or more years.

Contrary to the common stereotype of the black family as matriarchal, Hill's data suggest that most black families, whether low income or not, are characterized by an egalitarian pattern in which neither spouse dominates, that is, each shares in decision making and the performance of expected tasks. Moreover, national earnings data do not support the popular notion that wives' earnings in most low-income black families are often greater than those of their husbands. Recent Bureau of Labor statistics data indicate that in 85 percent of the black families with incomes under $3,000, the husband's earnings surpassed the wife's. Thus, contrary to the stereotype of black men as weak, irresponsible, and peripheral, the husband is the main provider in the majority of black families, whether low income or not.

A final strength of the black family is its traditional orientation toward achievement, which can be seen in the large numbers of black college students. A demonstration of this is the fact that in recent years, three-fourths of the blacks enrolled in college came from families that had no college education.

We see that Hill's interpretation of the black family does not coincide with Moynihan's. Beginning from the question of what keeps the black family going in spite of the unique pressures bearing upon it, Hill avoids a portrayal of the black family as disorganized, pathological, and disintegrating. His technique of starting where the phenomena are, as opposed to where one thinks they should be, renders Hill's investigation more balanced than Moynihan's. Its basis is also more soundly ethnographic.

THE CONTEXT OF ETHNOCENTRISM

Hill's data suggest the following interpretation: The internal cohesiveness of the black family is increased by its existence in the embedded and oppressed subculture; such an existence produces bonds like those described which are not necessary in the wholistic culture.

It is appropriate to note here that ethnocentrism in social science research does not exist in a vacuum: It is comfortably ensconced in institutional racism. But in order to understand what is meant here by institutional racism, it is first necessary to define racism in the broad sense. Terry (1970) defines racism as

> . . . any activity by individuals, groups, institutions, or cultures that treats human beings unjustly because of color and rationalizes that treatment by attributing to them undesirable biological, psychological, social or cultural characteristics. (p. 41)

This definition is basically descriptive. Jones (1972) offers a more dynamic definition:

> Racism results from the transformation of race prejudices and/or ethnocentrism through the exercise of power against a racial group, defined as inferior by individuals and institutions, with the intentional or unintentional support of the entire culture. (p. 117)

Prejudice is defined as

> . . . the prior negative judgment of the members of a race or religion or the occupants of any significant social role, held in disregard of facts that contradict it. (p. 61)

Despite the differences in perspective, both definitions of racism involve essentially the same tripartite analysis, which constitutes the three basic spheres within which racism operates: the culture, its institutions, and the individual. Each successive sphere is more particularized. Any analysis of racism must carefully examine each sphere and its implications for adjacent levels.

Individual racism taken by itself is, as Jones sees it, no more than race prejudice. Institutional racism manifests itself in labor relations, the legal system, human rights issues, health care, economics, education, politics, housing, etc. The racist consequences of the various kinds of institutions can be intentional or unintentional. Intentional racism is the institutionalization by the majority culture of such activities as poll tax and laws against intermarriage. Unintentional racism is a more subtle problem—functioning as it does among the middle and upper classes—that underlies the cultural assumptions upon which the institutions themselves are based. As Jones states:

> These assumptions form the bases of institutions which reward individuals insofar as they possess cultural forms and modes of expression congruent with the institutions' value system. It is at this level of practice that most Americans have been insensitive to the problems of racial conflict. (p. 146)

Cultural racism is expressed through racist conceptions and in formulations about aesthetics, religion, music, philosophy, values, needs, and beliefs and encompasses the other two categories. It permeates the value system of the culture that is the basis of its institutions. It is through these institutions that the individual members of society are socialized.

The relation of these three spheres—individual, institutional, and cultural—to each other is not linear but circular. Institutions generate and reinforce expressions of individual racism. The expressions of individuals within institutions feed back to reinforce the basic character of society. The cultural character is, moreover, a factor in the establishment of institutions which, in turn, socialize individuals. Thus the cycle persists. Racism abides on all three levels in various guises, thereby perpetuating itself. Given this condition, it should be apparent how ethnocentrism in social science research arises and persists.

In sharp contrast to the cultural deficit model, which evaluates minority behavior patterns against those of the majority, is one that can be labeled the *cultural difference model*. It asserts that the behavior patterns of black Americans are not the result of pathology, deficits, or genetic inferiority but rather the manifestations of a viable subculture which is complexly related to the total culture. The development of this subculture can be traced historically as a synthesis of African, colonial, and contemporary American cultures.

Cultural difference does not provide an easy solution to the problem of how behavior patterns observed in black Americans should be explained. It does, however, open the way for the development of a model that offers the most promise, that is, through the concept of *cultural pluralism*. A model of cultural difference would incorporate the major strains from minority life and those from mainstream cultural life, ascribing equal validity to each qualitatively.

Our main thrust in this book will be to demonstrate that the apparent racial differences in such cognitive matters as test taking, school learning, and speech patterns can best be explained by cultural phenomena, in particular, the subcultural experience. Our thesis throughout is that behavioral differences stem not from gene pool variations but from cultural ones.

SUMMARY

In this part we have illustrated how the wholistic cultural experience contrasts with the subcultural one. We have argued that cognitive functioning is differentially affected by an individual's experience within both cultures. We pointed out that the social science literature necessary for an explication of the subcultural experience has been ethnocentric. The difficulties this has posed for developing a theory about the subcultural experience have led us to a critical review of several social scientists' views of the black American. Our review suggests the necessity for an ethnographic method of explanation for understanding how the embedded subcultural experience differs from the wholistic culture experience.

The work cited in this part to illustrate ethnocentrism in social science research leaned heavily on fallacious interpretations of population statistics. It is therefore fruitful to inquire about relevant research emanating from other approaches that may also be subject to the label of ethnocentrism. In the remainder of the book we review some studies relevant to the black subcultural experience in the United States. Our review covers the following areas:

1. sociolinguistics
2. intellectual functioning and problem solving
3. self-concept

These three areas have been selected because they are central in social science research on black Americans.

SOCIOLINGUISTICS

Linguists who focus primarily on the social aspects and pragmatic use of language are known as sociolinguists. The field of sociolinguistics has become extremely important in recent years. Some researchers in this field have argued that the Chomskian emphasis on language universals (especially syntactic ones) has misdirected our understanding about the nature of language. The same researchers emphasize language performance, as opposed to language competence abstracted from performance. Hymes's (1973) account in some sense seeks to unite the concepts of competence and performance through investigation of the ethnography of language use. He deals with performance competence in terms of a user's knowledge of the phonology, syntax, and lexicon appropriate to a particular social and topical setting. This approach is more fruitful when one seeks to ascertain how subcultural groups differ from each other or from the wholistic culture.

Another reason for reviewing language studies about the subcultural experience is that the political and economic bases of oppressed minorities often overtly get expressed as concern over the language differences of these groups (see

Ferguson, 1973). That is, even though language differences per se appear not to be the sole reason for justifying continued oppression in the culture, many conflicts across cultures seem to imply this. Consequently, it is rewarding to survey the sociolinguistic literature with an eye toward extracting those generalizations that will shed light on the subcultural experience. It should be kept in mind that although language is the means by which researchers extract these generalizations, the goal we have in mind goes beyond language. In fact, we see language (for example, dialects) as a related aspect of a larger phenomenon—subcultural embedding.

Three categories of language aspect will be treated here:

1. structure
2. content
3. function

Some of the studies reviewed in each section were undertaken with an applied focus while others to be reviewed have a purely theoretical orientation. Our focus is on those portions of sociolinguistics that deal with the black English vernacular (BEV).

A highly condensed list of the features of BEV that will be frequently referred to in the subsequent review is presented in Table 1.

STRUCTURE

Linguistic Structure and Applications

Phonology

A sizable body of literature exists on phonology and grammar as they relate to reading interference among BEV

TABLE 1

Features of black English vernacular (BEV)

1. Variations in phonology

   a. *th* changed to *t, d, f, v*

*th*ing	ting
no*th*ing	nofing
*th*en	den
ba*th*e	bave

   b. Final consonants reduced, deleted

mo*m*	ma	(nasalized)
boo*t*	boo	(glottal stop)
fee*d*	feet	(devoiced)
roa*d*	roa	
ki*ss*	ki	(weakened)
ha*s*	ha	
ma*n*	ma	(nasalized)
ki*ck*	ki	(glottal stop)
ga*g*	gak	(devoiced)
ba*g*	bay	(devoiced)

   c. *L* deleted

to*l*l	toe
he*l*p	hep

   d. *R* replaced or deleted

so*r*e	so
ma*rr*y	may

   e. Consonant clusters simplified

*s*tream	scream	pa*st*	pass
*s*hrimp	simp	mi*nd*	mine
*th*row	thow	si*ft*	sif
professo*r*	pofessa	sol*d*	sow
		va*ts*	vas

Note. From "Black dialect interference and accommodation of reading instruction in first grade" by A. Piestrup, *Language-Behavior Research Laboratory*, 1973, 176–178, University of California, Berkeley. (Monograph No. 4)

TABLE 1

Features of black English vernacular (BEV) *(continued)*

---

  f. Vowels modified

f*ear*	f*are*	r*aw*	r*ow*
p*in*	p*en*	t*ime*	t*om*
p*oor*	p*ore*	j*oy*	j*aw*
s*ure*	sh*ore*	pr*oud*	pr*od*

2. Variations in morphology

  a. Plural

tests	tesez
men	mens
kittens	kitten

  b. Possessive

Tom's book	Tom book
their friend	they friend

  c. Third person singular present

she talks	she talk
he is	he be
he has	he have
he does	he do

  d. Past tense

passed	pass

  e. Irregular verb classes

I said	I say
he takes	he taken
He is sick.	He be sick.
He isn't here.	He ain't here.

  f. Auxiliary verbs

Fred'll be coming.	Fred be coming.

  g. Comparative adjectives

She's smarter.	She more smarter.

3. Variations in syntax

  a. Adjectives used as adverbs

  He talks real good.

TABLE 1

Features of black English vernacular (BEV) *(continued)*

---

b. Pronoun variation

My father, he walk sharp.

c. Assignment to word classes: have, be, do

I got me a tow truck.
I been there.

d. Patterns — habitual action

He will be sick.   He sick.

e. Count nouns and mass nouns

I seen three police.

f. Prepositional phrases

That there child

g. Modal modification

They useta could beat ya.

h. Future markers

I'm a throw it.
He be comin' tommorrow.

i. Transformations of "there," negative questions, passive.

They a lot of people here.
I ain't care.
Nobody won't do nothing.
Can't nobody help you.
Why you don't know?
How they know?

j. Clauses: noun, adjectival

I don't know is he there.
The place where I lived at.

---

speakers. Generally speaking, the distinction between grammatical and phonological features of BEV is not clearcut. Simons (1973) has noted the following:

First, there are features that are wholly phonological such as a consonant cluster simplification in monomorphemic words, e.g., "test,"—"tess," "desk"—"dess." Second, there are features that are phonological in origin but intersect with consonant cluster simplification in words with past tense morphemes, e.g., "liked"—"like," "passed"—"pass," etc. Third, there are features that are clearly grammatical such as the invariant "be."

In a study bearing on the question of phonological interference, Melamed (1971) compared third-grade black children with third-grade white children on their ability to discriminate auditorily, to produce, to comprehend in oral reading, and to comprehend in silent reading the phonological features of "r-lessness"–"l-lessness," consonant cluster simplification, weakening of final consonants, and vowel variations. These are the major phonological features in which BEV differs from standard English (SE). He found that the black children differed from the white children in auditory discrimination and production of the selected features. The blacks failed to discriminate the features and did not produce them as frequently as the whites did. This difference thus served to demonstrate that the blacks were dialect speakers and the whites were not. If phonological interference exists, speakers who exhibit the greatest amount of dialect features should do less well on the reading measures than those who do not. If there is no phonological interference, then there should be no difference in the reading measures. The latter was found to be the case for Melamed's subjects. The black subjects differed on auditory discrimination and production of the selected phonological features, but they did not differ on their ability to comprehend them in oral and silent reading. Melamed's findings, as well as his interpretation, find support in Shuy's (1973) recent discussion of the question of phonological interference and reading performance as it relates to children from BEV-speaking communities.

Rystrom (1970) reports on another study bearing on the question of phonological interference. He examined the question of such interference by conducting an experiment in which he compared the effect of training in the production of SE phonology on the reading achievement of BEV speakers. The experimental group received training in producing SE phonology, and the control group received language arts training without particular emphasis on SE phonology. He found that neither training in SE phonology nor type of reading instruction produced significant differences on four measures of reading achievement.

Further indirect evidence on the question of phonological interference is provided by Osterberg (1961), who studied reading acquisition in an area of Sweden where the prestige dialect is not spoken. He conducted an experiment in which a group of first-grade children were taught for the first ten weeks of the school year with books especially written to conform to the phonological features of the dialect area in which they lived. A control group received instruction using standard texts that conform to the standard Swedish speech. If phonological interference with learning to read exists, then teaching students to read with texts that conform to their phonological system should reduce this interference and thus increase reading achievement. If this line of reasoning is correct, then the experimental group in the Osterberg study should have learned to read better than the control group. Osterberg found that the experimental group was superior to the control group after ten weeks and at the end of one year, on various measures of reading achievement.

Taken as a whole, the evidence on phonological interference in learning to read is inconsistent; hence, the questions about phonological interference must remain open.

Syntax

It has been suggested by Stewart (1969) and Baratz (1969) that a major reason why BEV speakers achieve poorly in reading is the difference between their grammar and the SE grammar of instructional reading materials. In the case of grammar, the interference presumably would be with reading comprehension.

There are two major ways in which BEV syntax can hamper reading comprehension. First, it can influence interpretation in cases where the SE sentence is incorrectly seen as an equivalent BEV sentence. One example presented by Stewart (1969) is the SE sentence, "His eye's open," which may be interpreted by the BEV speaker to mean that both eyes are open because it resembles the BEV sentence "His eyes open" more than it does "His eye open," the latter being the BEV equivalent of "His eye's open." Another example, also pointed out by Stewart, is the interpretation of "He will be busy" as implying habitual action, because "be" in BEV can be used as a marker for habitual action.

The second, less direct kind of potential interference arises as a result of the difference between BEV and SE syntax. Even when the BEV speaker is able to translate an SE phrase into the equivalent BEV form, the process itself may place on the BEV speaker the burden of taking an extra step when going from the text printed in SE to the meaning. That is, whatever may be the precise procedure involved in translating print into meaning, it is reasonable to assume that both the SE and BEV speakers, at some point in the process, must do a syntactic analysis of the written sentence. This analysis is based on SE syntax. The BEV speaker must perform an additional analysis of translation, which requires an extra step. The steps accumulate over the stretch of large amounts of reading to the point where comprehension is interfered with.

Additional evidence on the question of indirect grammatical interference is provided by Ruddell (1963) and Tatham (1970). Both found that SE-speaking, white elementary school children comprehended material written in grammatical sentence patterns more frequently used in their oral language better than material written in sentence patterns less frequently used. This finding illustrates one aspect of an ethnographic approach, namely, the relative frequency with which language patterns are employed naturalistically. (On this point, see also Rentel & Kennedy, 1972, and Sims, 1972.)

Further evidence of the question of grammatical interference is provided by Garvey and McFarlane (1970). They correlated the number of deviations from SE produced by fifth-grade students on a sentence-repetition task with reading achievement. Each of the sentences on the task contained structures that are conflict points between SE and BEV. They used three groups of children: lower-class blacks, lower-class whites, and middle-class whites. They found correlations of .03, −.53 and −.72, respectively, between the sentence-repetition task and reading achievement for the three groups. The correlations for the lower- and middle-class white groups are statistically significant, but that for the lower-class black group is not.

Labov (1970) attempted to determine directly the degree of interference produced by a particular grammatical feature, the past-tense morpheme -ed. BEV speakers typically fail to pronounce this morpheme. The question is, do they understand that the -ed signals past tense? If they do not, then their comprehension of the sentence might be impaired, which would be a case of direct interference. In an ingenious experiment designed to answer the question, Labov asked junior high school BEV speakers to read aloud sentences like the following: "When I passed by, I read the posters. I looked for trouble when I read the news." Their pronunciation of the homograph *read* was to be an indication of whether or not they understood the *-ed* of *passed* and *looked* to be a past-tense marker 35 percent to 55 percent of the time. This fact suggests that failure to pronounce the *-ed* interfered with comprehension more than half the time.

In a more detailed analysis, Labov compared subjects' sensitivity to the grammatical or the phonological constraints on consonant cluster simplifications and its effects on reading the *-ed* suffix. He found that subjects who were more sensitive to grammatical constraints read the *-ed* words correctly more often than did subjects who were more sensitive to the phonological constraints or subjects who were equally sensitive to both constraints. Thus, subjects who deleted the *-ed* less often, regardless of whether the following word began with a consonant or a vowel, were better readers of the test sentence.

Possible Educational Implications

Given the data presented, it appears that the hypotheses about phonological and grammatical interference may have to be revised. It may be that black dialect does not interfere with the acquisition of reading skills for all black dialect speakers in all educational situations. Indeed, Piestrup (1973) has shown that the ways teachers communicate in the classroom are crucial to a child's success in learning to read. Moreover, she states that

> . . . efforts to find deficits in children or to focus on their language differences may only confound the problems of negative teacher expectations and evade the problem of functional conflict between teachers and children with different cultural backgrounds. Teachers can alienate children from learning by subtly rejecting their black

speech. They can discourage them by implying by tone, gesture and even by silence that the children lack potential. Children, in turn, can show their resilience by engaging in verbal play and ritual insult apart from the teacher, or they can withdraw into a moody silence. Neither strategy helps them to learn to read.

From a review of the literature, and especially the Piestrup study, we again see the importance of carrying out ethnographic investigations of the special function of language in terms of the subcultural experience, i.e., functional conflict between teachers and BEV students is directly accounted for by a mismatch in communication skills. Further insights into the nature of this mismatch could be gained by a more thorough ethnographic investigation.

Summary

Sociolinguists have argued for a reinterpretation of language competence from the point of view of the social functions of language. This emphasis is especially important in studying the language function of a group such as black Americans because it requires the interpreter to refer observed differences in phonology, morphology, syntax, and function to their source in the cultural experience.

Some scholars regard BEV as a creole formed originally from contact of African slaves with their white overseers. The original language, a pidgin, over generations of transmission gradually became a more systematic and enriched form of language, which scholars then term a creole. Depending upon which region of the country one focuses on, BEV reflects differing degrees of influence in terms of what forces and which social groups shaped it into its present form.

One BEV, a northern variety, has been studied by numerous linguists. Their studies reveal an internally consistent language which follows its own system of phonological, morphological, and syntactic rules. In addition, there are differences in the function that BEV serves in the black community; this section has surveyed some possible implications that these differences may have for education.

One hypothesis discussed suggests that phonological interference will increase reading difficulty because texts follow the language forms of the dominant culture. This requires some form of cognitive adjustment for the reader whose preferred and more familiar language is BEV. The data to date suggest conflicting findings regarding the effect of a possible phonological conflict for learning to read. Of course, in none of the work from which the data were derived were motivation, setting, and cultural dominance controlled.

Another hypothesis also examined has to do with some possible educational implications of being a BEV speaker, namely, mismatching in syntactic systems the language of the majority and minority cultures. It was assumed that translation across dialects is required for BEV speakers to understand SE texts. If this is so, then an additional cognitive load is placed on BEV speakers who read such materials that were designed with SE users in mind. The evidence here is more persuasive.

But again, studies that focus on language forms per se miss much of the source of difficulty in learning to read. The educational setting can dramatically influence the ease of learning to read, as a study by Piestrup has shown. Functional conflicts between teacher and students who come from different cultural backgrounds may be a key contribution to such difficulty.

Cognitive Structure and Dialect

To investigate some relationships between cognitive structure and dialect, Hall and Freedle (1973) studied whether blacks and whites do better when recalling sentences within one dialect or the other (SE or BEV). A total of 360 subjects, an equal number of males and females, were used in their experiment. One half the subjects were from the lower socioeconomic group and the other half from the middle socioeconomic group, as determined by the Hollingshead scale (Hollingshead & Redlich, 1958). The subjects were distributed equally in groups of 15 by three age categories (5, 8, and 10) in the aforementioned classifications. Each subject was required to listen to stimulus sentences, one half of them given in SE and the other half in BEV. These two types of sentences were randomly distributed throughout the task. The responses of each subject were tape-recorded and scored for the presence of the following structures (see Baratz, 1969):

1. third-person singular
2. presence of copula
3. negation
4. *if* + subject + verb
5. past markers
6. possessive marker
7. plural
8. nonaddition of third-person singular
9. zero copula
10. double negation and *ain't*
11. zero *if* + verb + subject
12. zero past morpheme
13. zero possessive morpheme
14. use of *be*

Examples of these types can be found in the first eight entries of Table 2.

TABLE 2

Some examples of syntactic differences between
standard English and black English vernacular

Variable	SE	BEV
Linking verb (copula)	He *is* going.	He _ goin'.
Possessive marker	John*'s* cousin.	John_ cousin.
Plural marker	I have five cent*s*.	I got five cent_.
Third-person singular (verb agreement)	He live*s* in New York.	He live_ in New York.
Past marker	Yesterday he walk*ed* home.	Yesterday he walk_ home.
"If" construction	I asked *if he did it.*	I ask *did he do it.*
Negation	I *don't* have *any.*	I *don't* got *none.*
Use of "be"	Statement: He is here *all the time.*	Statement: He *be* here.
Subject expression	John moved.	John, *he* move.
Verb form	I *drank* the milk.	I *drunk* the milk.
Future form	I *will go* home.	I*'ma go* home.
Indefinite article	I want *an* apple.	I want *a* apple.
Pronoun form	*We* have to do it.	*Us* got to do it.
Pronoun expressing possession	*His* book.	*He* book.
Preposition	He is over *at* John's house.	He over *to* John house.
	He teaches *at* Francis Pool.	He teaches _ Francis Pool.
Use of "do"	Contradiction: No, he *isn't.*	Contradiction: No, he *don't.*

Note. Adapted from "A bidialectal task for determining language proficiency in economically disadvantaged children" by Joan C. Baratz, *Child Development*, 1969, 3(40), 889–901.

Hall and Freedle reasoned that the ability to respond correctly to structures from within the same dialect should yield a positive correlation. If all paired structures from within a dialect are positively correlated, one might say that the two dialects represent a coherent linguistic system.

When structures are correlated across dialects, negative correlations seem to indicate cognitive interference across the dialects as distinct systems. But the results were somewhat more complicated than originally anticipated. The data from the Hall and Freedle study of 8- and 10-year-olds are presented in Tables 3 and 4.

Table 3 shows the paired correlations of each structure (seven SE and seven BEV structures) with every other structure. In the top triangular matrix are the correlations for the lower-class blacks; and just below are the entries for the middle-class blacks. Thus, for example, the correlation of the standard third-person singular with the standard copula as calculated from the black lower-class blacks is .69. The lower triangular matrix presents the intercorrelations for all 8-year-old blacks, and the entry just below gives that for the 10-year-old blacks. Consequently, .67 is the correlation of standard copula with standard third-person singular for the 8-year-old black subjects; that for the 10-year-olds is .38. Comparable data for white subjects are given in Table 4.

Examination of each of these triangular matrices reveals a very consistent pattern. The correlations of standard constructions with each are almost always positive. Similarly, the intercorrelation of BEV constructions with other BEV constructions is also virtually always positive. Thus the original hypothesis is confirmed here. On the other hand, when one examines the correlations across dialects, one finds that a large number, but not all, tend to be negative. For

TABLE 3

Intercorrelation of seven SE and seven BEV forms for 8- and 10-year-old lower- and middle-class blacks

SE forms	Standard structures							Nonstandard structures						
	3rd	Cop	Neg	If	Past	Poss	Plur	3rd	Cop	Neg	If	Past	Poss	Be
3rd		.59	.51	.35	.38	.59	.62	-.31	.27	.25	-.09	.02	.19	.34
		.69	.64	.52	.57	.54	.67	-.28	.34	.42	-.08	.10	.13	.33
Cop	.67		.32	.26	.35	.46	.56	.01	.33	.37	-.06	.11	.12	.38
	.38		.61	.41	.50	.60	.74	.08	.31	.52	.11	.38	.25	.43
Neg	.63	.62		.03	.26	.53	.26	-.25	.14	.07	-.02	.01	.14	.05
	.43	.13		.47	.53	.47	.54	-.02	.28	.30	-.06	.13	.14	.18
If	.35	.31	.28		.20	.25	.25	-.23	.17	.11	-.42	.11	-.14	.05
	.47	.26	.18		.41	.36	.36	.06	.28	.24	-.54	.33	.09	.29
Past	.54	.62	.45	.30		.31	.36	.01	.08	.15	-.07	.12	.00	.07
	.34	-.05	.27	.34		.32	.52	-.16	.14	.32	-.07	-.05	.12	.06
Poss	.57	.55	.53	.22	.33		.33	-.30	.01	.22	-.28	-.03	-.02	.04
	.45	.35	.39	.32	.27		.50	-.04	.33	.40	-.07	.33	.02	.24
Plur	.58	.75	.45	.28	.52	.32		.00	.32	.35	.10	.13	.11	.35
	.54	.26	.19	.23	.21	.37		.06	.28	.51	.20	.18	.15	.43

46

BEV forms

Form		1	2	3	4	5	6	7	8	9	10	11	12	13
3rd		-.19	.15	-.03	-.04	.12	-.08	.24	.04	.34	.41	.18	.14	.19
		-.56	-.11	-.27	-.16	-.45	-.32	-.26	.17	.23	.09	.33	.20	.40
Cop		.29	.37	.26	.14	.12	.23	.35		.56	.23	.22	.07	.31
		.20	.19	.09	.20	.01	.02	.18		.36	-.02	.31	.22	.43
Neg		.42	.51	.27	.14	.33	.37	.50	.49		.27	.39	.19	.45
		-.20	.04	-.17	-.04	-.13	-.07	.02	.45		-.06	.32	.44	.56
If		-.07	.19	-.03	-.33	.10	-.11	.29	.31	.18		.28	.25	.19
		-.29	-.22	-.13	-.71	-.43	-.32	-.04	-.05	.11		-.05	-.04	-.02
Past		.02	.35	.26	.15	.13	.27	.20	.33	.32	.30		.42	.16
		-.19	-.07	-.24	.15	-.21	-.08	-.10	.20	.33	-.01		.26	.40
Poss		.22	.26	.18	-.03	.17	.15	.15	.16	.21	.22	.35		.32
		-.24	-.22	-.08	-.26	-.27	-.42	-.17	.12	.28	.18	.30		.41
Be		.37	.43	.23	.06	.19	.19	.41	.48	.50	.19	.26	.36	—
		.01	.21	-.16	.11	-.28	-.12	.22	.27	.45	.06	.28	.32	—

Note. Each correlation is based on $N = 60$. In the upper triangular matrix the value from the lower class is above that of the middle class; in the lower triangular matrix, the 8-year-olds' data are above the 10-year-olds' data.

TABLE 4

Intercorrelation of seven SE and seven BEV forms for 8- and 10-year-old lower- and middle-class whites

SE forms	Standard structures							Nonstandard structures						
	3rd	Cop	Neg	If	Past	Poss	Plur	3rd	Cop	Neg	If	Past	Poss	Be
3rd		.69	.56	.60	.58	.60	.70	.04	.19	.25	-.14	.11	.10	.46
		.56	.56	.40	.50	.49	.43	-.16	.00	.17	-.20	-.04	.21	.03
Cop	.71		.50	.42	.67	.64	.57	.09	.22	.36	.09	.16	.08	.30
	.55		.47	.22	.40	.53	.45	.10	.15	.35	.08	.01	.27	.06
Neg	.54	.42		.55	.38	.40	.46	.09	.13	.18	-.20	-.04	.19	.29
	.54	.55		.41	.35	.35	.29	.00	.08	-.10	-.22	.05	.23	.04
If	.51	.40	.49		.50	.35	.52	.10	.05	.24	-.43	.02	-.08	.34
	.65	.29	.42		.39	.32	.20	.00	.12	.01	-.47	-.05	.14	-.01
Past	.67	.70	.34	.53		.51	.67	.12	.09	.37	.08	.17	.08	.22
	.29	.34	.33	.30		.38	.40	-.16	-.05	.09	-.23	-.01	.23	.02
Poss	.59	.69	.36	.34	.59		.58	-.06	.18	.11	.00	.03	.06	.38
	.62	.52	.45	.49	.26		.30	.10	.15	.30	-.02	-.02	.16	.13
Plur	.66	.58	.34	.46	.70	.58		.15	.18	.47	-.08	.11	.09	.37
	.53	.41	.39	.30	.27	.40		.15	.22	.30	.02	.13	.34	.10

BEV forms

	(1)	(2)	(3)	(4)	(5)	(6)	(7)	3rd	Cop	Neg	If	Past	Poss	Be
3rd	-.17 / -.10	-.02 / .04	.06 / -.14	.15 / -.27	.06 / -.23	-.06 / -.04	.06 / .05		.26 / .58	.24 / .46	.03 / .31	.18 / .44	.23 / .50	.14 / .55
Cop	.02 / .20	.10 / .28	.05 / .14	.10 / .05	.03 / .04	.12 / .24	.20 / .18	.33 / .45		.38 / .34	.02 / .22	.04 / .34	.37 / .33	.50 / .40
Neg	.19 / .13	.32 / .29	.04 / -.12	.15 / -.02	.26 / .12	.19 / .17	.35 / .30	.30 / .38	.20 / .43		-.03 / .09	.13 / .36	.12 / .54	.19 / .42
If	-.11 / -.33	.07 / -.02	-.27 / -.16	-.43 / -.55	.16 / -.39	.04 / -.20	.07 / -.36	-.02 / .31	.15 / .23	.03 / .02		.22 / .39	.24 / .19	-.02 / .22
Past	.01 / .03	.07 / .05	.00 / -.06	.03 / -.15	.11 / .03	.04 / -.04	.10 / .04	.14 / .38	.30 / .20	.30 / .20	.17 / .38		.07 / .33	.24 / .52
Poss	.17 / .14	.15 / .19	.20 / .22	.14 / -.10	.20 / .06	.12 / .14	.18 / .22	-.01 / .50	.19 / .40	.27 / .43	.03 / .29	-.02 / .33		.17 / .45
Be	.25 / .31	.15 / .27	.24 / .06	.25 / .13	.26 / -.03	.27 / .30	.22 / .31	.16 / .47	.30 / .54	.22 / .41	-.09 / .19	.43 / .37	.11 / .49	

Note. Each correlation is based on $N = 60$. In the upper triangular matrix the value from the lower class is above that of the middle class; in the lower triangular matrix, the 8-year-olds' data are above the 10-year-olds' data.

example, for the lower-class blacks, the correlation of standard "if" with BEV "if" is —.42. The same general tendency for negative correlations to occur across dialects can also be seen when examining the data from the white subjects.

This somewhat systematic effect can be interpreted as evidence that within a dialect, an internally consistent system of grammatical rules (and/or cognitive operations) produces positive correlations of every structure with every other structure in that same system. This leads us to assert that these behavioral data indicate the psychological reality of a BEV and a separate psychological reality of the SE dialect. This separateness is found even for speakers who know both dialects, as Table 3 clearly reveals for black subjects. Many of the negative correlations across dialects indicate that some mutual confusion may result when the speaker goes from one dialect system to another, even though it is a similar one. However, it should be noted that exceptions to this finding occurred. BEV copula, double negation, and use of *be* appear to be somewhat positively related across dialects. This does not contradict the assertion that BEV is an internally consistent dialect, however; it indicates rather that there are complex linkages across dialects.

Cognitive Change and Dialect

Since the Hall and Freedle report, additional analyses of their data have been conducted that furnish evidence that changes occur in the cognitive structuring of the dialect systems with age.

Using the sentence-recall task, Hall and Freedle (1973) found that the dialects of 8- and 10-year-olds are two linguistically distinct systems. The correlational evidence indicated that within a dialect, strong positive measures were obtained, but across dialects, negative, zero, and a few positive correlations occurred. We have now found what may be a surprising aspect of these data.

In four sets of results for the 5-year-olds (see Table 5) we find the following: black lower-class and white middle-class subjects tend to have predominantly high positive correlations both within each dialect and across dialects. (A few scattered negative correlations occur for the black lower-class subjects, but they are small in magnitude.) The correlations for black middle-class and white lower-class subjects tend to produce high positive correlations within and across dialects, but the negative correlations seem to be somewhat larger and more systematically arranged when they appear across dialects. For the black middle-class subjects, we note that most of the negative correlations occur for BEV "Cop" in comparison with the SE forms, but for the white lower-class subjects, the negative correlations involve BEV "If" in comparison with all the SE forms (and even some of the other BEV forms).

Before we begin to speculate on the meaning of these differences, let us discuss in more detail the correlations of the 8- and 10-year-olds. When negative correlations appeared across dialects, they involved BEV "3rd" with standard forms (this was made evident for the black lower-class data). These negative relationships are not yet present, however, for the 5-year-olds.

For BEV "Cop" compared with SE forms, the 8- and 10-year-olds show positive correlations for blacks and whites of both socioeconomic levels. For 5-year-olds, BEV "Cop" produces negative correlations across SE forms for primarily the black middle-class subjects.

BEV "Neg" remains fairly constant (positive) across age, race, and socioeconomic level within and across dialects.

BEV "If" is strongly negative for the 8- and 10-year-olds across dialect systems for blacks, whites, and lower- and

TABLE 5

Five-year-olds' sentence recall data for two dialects

	SE						BEV					
	3rd	Cop	Neg	If	Poss	Pl	3rd	Cop	Neg	If	Poss	Be
SE												
3rd	**1.00**	.51	.50	.29	.40	.36	-.31	-.03	-.01	.04	.32	.08
Cop	.46	**1.00**	.70	.44	.29	.63	.00	-.26	.11	.06	.41	.12
Neg	.43	.64	**1.00**	.25	.04	.41	.08	-.06	.30	-.10	.44	.08
If	.32	.33	.30	**1.00**	.39	.31	.18	-.18	.16	.00	.08	.13
Poss	.47	.18	.19	.39	**1.00**	.33	-.04	-.09	.12	-.13	.06	.26
Pl	.36	.77	.58	.26	.34	**1.00**	-.29	-.17	-.04	.14	.24	.13
BEV												
3rd	.13	.44	.25	.21	.12	.31	**1.00**	.17	.58	-.18	.09	.50
Cop	.15	-.07	.10	.21	.03	.10	.31	**1.00**	.37	.12	.28	.39
Neg	.39	.44	.16	.34	.37	.47	.60	.46	**1.00**	-.02	.18	.55
If	.38	.38	.15	-.18	.27	.29	.35	-.07	.31	**1.00**	.24	.04
Poss	.24	.19	.31	-.10	.07	.15	.34	-.04	-.05	.29	**1.00**	.33
Be	.42	.18	.26	.11	.16	.20	.49	.34	.41	.14	.38	**1.00**

Note. Black middle class above diagonal boldface numbers; black lower class below diagonal boldface numbers.

SE

	3rd	Cop	Neg	If	Poss	Pl	3rd	Cop	Neg	If	Poss	Be
3rd	**1.00**	.65	.50	.42	.47	.57	.30	.08	.19	.00	.15	.20
Cop	.65	**1.00**	.81	.74	.65	.76	.50	.10	.52	.00	.40	.50
Neg	.51	.64	**1.00**	.62	.58	.71	.40	.10	.46	.00	.26	.39
If	.61	.47	.40	**1.00**	.50	.65	.38	.24	.42	.00	.36	.43
Poss	.28	.42	.26	.25	**1.00**	.72	.17	.32	.44	.00	.37	.48
Pl	.44	.61	.64	.50	.35	**1.00**	.40	.17	.46	.00	.28	.44

BEV

	3rd	Cop	Neg	If	Poss	Pl	3rd	Cop	Neg	If	Poss	Be
3rd	.44	.50	.36	.52	.27	.64	**1.00**	.23	.67	.00	.24	.23
Cop	.05	.25	.34	.25	-.11	.20	.35	**1.00**	.21	.00	.35	.49
Neg	.23	.03	.06	.30	.03	.16	.37	.41	**1.00**	.00	.39	.25
If	-.21	-.23	-.17	-.15	-.12	-.18	-.19	-.11	-.15	**1.00**	.00	.00
Poss	.44	.37	.31	.55	.55	.21	.37	-.02	.15	-.08	**1.00**	.50
Be	.09	.37	.27	.03	.39	.04	-.04	.10	-.33	-.10	.18	**1.00**

Note. White middle class above diagonal boldface numbers; white lower class below diagonal boldface numbers.

middle-class subjects in general. It is negative at age 5 only for the white lower class. Across systems, it tends to be zero and mildly positive for white and black middle-class 5-year-olds, but predominantly positive for 5-year-old black lower-class subjects.

BEV "Poss" is strongly positive across dialects for all 5-year-olds and only moderately positive for all 8- and 10-year-olds, regardless of race or socioeconomic status.

BEV "be" across dialects tends to be positive for all age, race, and socioeconomic status groups.

Even though this tangle of results may defy any simple interpretation, there are apparent differences that surely have a meaning.

If we focus only on the data for 5-year-olds and ignore further changes over age groups, the results suggest that most of the correlations within and across dialects are positive. One possible interpretation of this is that the 5-year-olds have learned a single cognitive-language system which unites the dialects by a common set of rules. The 5-year-olds apply this single system to control their sentence recall regardless of the input sentence, be it BEV or SE.

The differentiation of the two dialects into separate behavioral systems (as suggested by the overall data from the 8- and 10-year olds) might then be explained as a result of exposure to the school system, where a single dialect tends to be used. The contrast of the school system's language with the hypothetically undifferentiated language of the preschool years facilitates the cognitive distinctiveness of the two systems.

Summary

The conditions under which one learns a language system and its dialects (variants) influence the way the language structures are organized in memory. When they are learned in a unicultural environment where they function somewhat interchangeably (with perhaps some situations being totally committed to one form, as in "playing the dozens"—which, in Harlem, is tied to BEV only), they appear to be organized as a single cognitive system. Later, when the individuals using the dual systems become exposed increasingly to outside communities whose language functions and rules are noticeably different, the individuals appear to cognitively separate SE and BEV into distinct systems which have only partial interconnections (positive correlations for only some pairs of grammatical forms). The effect of the environment appears to be responsible for this cognitive restructuring.

CONTENT

Vocabulary

Test Performance and Dialect

The data in the category of vocabulary are probably the scantiest of all (see, for example, Cazden, 1972). This is especially true when we speak of vocabulary as content. It appears that poor minority group children consistently show slower lexical development than other children, as measured by

1. vocabulary subtests of IQ tests such as the Wechsler Intelligence Scale for Children (WISC); see, for example, Shuey, 1966
2. level of syntactic responding in Entwistle-type free-association tests
3. recognition vocabulary tests such as the Peabody

Some data, however, have been reported on the question of vocabulary and BEV by Williams and Rivers (1972). They

TABLE 6

Total class means, standard deviations,
and difference scores from SE and
BEV performance data

	Group		
	SE	BEV	Difference
M	32.259	35.594	3.335*
SD	16.941	18.218	1.277
N	495.	945.	

Note. Adapted from "Mismatches in testing from black English" by R. Williams and W. Rivers. Paper presented at the annual meeting of the American Psychological Association, Honolulu, 1972.
*$t = 2.98$ significant at .01 level.

investigated score changes on the Boehm Test of Basic Concepts (BTBC) as a function of changes in the vocabulary of the test in the direction of BEV, having hypothesized that under conditions of a fair predictor (the BTBC under BEV instructions) a black child would perform significantly better than under those of an unfair predictor (the BTBC under SE instructions). To test this hypothesis, three studies were done, employing SE and BEV versions of the BTBC.

The first study dealt with 990 black kindergarten and first- and second-grade children from 48 classrooms. Race, IQ, age, sex, and grade level were controlled for. Testing was done in the classroom by either a black teacher or a black graduate student, each of whom possessed expert control of BEV expressions. A short form of the WISC was administered to 125 randomly selected children from each group. The classrooms were randomly assigned to SE or BEV testing conditions, with an average of 20 students per classroom.

Mean and standard deviation scores from the performances of the experimental and control classes are shown in Table 6.

As one can see from the table, the mean score of the BEV classes is significantly higher than that of the SE classes. These results support the hypothesis regarding the differential sensitivity of the BEV, or dialect-fair, instructions.

In a second study, 59 children from kindergarten and first- and second-grades from three classrooms were selected for investigation. The purpose of the study was to chart the performance of children from families belonging to the lower socioeconomic level. None of the subjects in the study had participated in the first study.

Tests of significance were performed at each grade level to test the hypothesis of differential sensitivity of the BEV version of the BTBC. These results can be seen in Table 7. Here we can see that levels of BEV performance are significantly different from those of SE performance at each grade level. The greatest mean difference occurs at the kindergarten level. In both studies, BEV presentation produced the highest performance scores.

TABLE 7

Comparisons between SE and BEV performance on the BTBC Form A by grade level

	Kindergarten		Grade 1		Grade 2	
	SE	BEV	SE	BEV	SE	BEV
M	25.95*	36.94	39.55*	45.30	42.33	46.55
SD	6.63	9.22	3.46	2.45	4.59	3.74
t ratio	3.95*		9.839*		3.154*	
N	19		19		20	

*Significant at .01.

The third, and final, study focused on a comparison of the performance of subjects in the second study with normative data reported in the Boehm test manual (see Tables 8 and 9). We can see here the mean differences between the data presented by Boehm and the results of the presentation of her standard version in this study are not statistically significant. Differences were found when the

TABLE 8

A comparison of Boehm's original reliability sample data with the Williams and Rivers data

	Boehm data reliability sample ($N = 2,647$) by grade and socioeconomic level (Form A)			Williams and Rivers data ($N = 59$) by grade and treatment for lower-class subjects (Form A)	
	(1) Low	(2) Middle	(3) High	(4) Standard	(5) BEV
Kindergarten					
N	162	453	250	19	19
M	28.4	35.3	39.4	25.95	36.94
SD	8.1	8.0	6.5	6.63	9.22
Grade 1					
N	276	413	280	19	19
M	39.2	43.8	45.6	39.55	45.30
SD	5.0	4.5	3.7	3.46	2.45
Grade 2					
N	222	349	242	21	21
M	43.5	46.7	47.8	42.33	46.55
SD	5.0	4.5	2.6	4.59	3.74

Note. Adapted from "Mismatches in testing from black English" by R. Williams and W. Rivers. Paper presented at the annual meeting of the American Psychological Association, Honolulu, 1972. Used with permission.

TABLE 9

T scores based on comparisons of mean scores from
Boehm's reliability sample and those from the
Williams and Rivers exploratory data

	Socioeconomic level		
	Low	Middle	High
Kindergarten			
SE	1.450	5.807	8.302*
BEV	3.769*	.743	1.050
Grade 1			
SE	.887	5.024	7.151*
BEV	9.342*	2.483†	.497
Grade 2			
SE	1.083	4.218*	5.260*
BEV	3.312*	.172	1.430

*Significant at the .05 and .01 levels.
†Significant at the .05 level.

means of the BEV version presentations were compared with
those reported by Boehm for the low socioeconomic groups.
It is interesting to note the similarity between the data
derived from Boehm's upper socioeconomic groups and that
derived from the BEV version presentations to lower-class
children. In some cases, the BEV treatment produced
performance scores which exceeded those achieved by both
middle and high socioeconomic groups in the Boehm
normative sample.

It has already been suggested in the discussion of the data
from Hall and Freedle (1973) that experience in the
subcultural community definitely affects the evaluation of
the dialects as separate systems. Thus, dialect mediates as
well as reflects differences in subcultural experience.

Language here clearly makes a difference: it is the means by which one can infer subcultural difference. Likewise, Williams and Rivers (1972) find that language makes a difference in test performance. Mismatch in dialect used in test administration and the one preferred by the examinee leads to an underestimation of vocabulary knowledge of SE. We infer that this difference may be due to true subcultural differences in the meanings of words.

Summary

Williams and Rivers (1972) found the following. First, there were significant differences between the mean performance scores of children who were administered the SE version of the BTBC and children who were administered a BEV version. Children taking the dialect-fair version scored significantly higher than did those who received the SE version. Second, the mean scores obtained from the performance of the subjects in the St. Louis sample on the BEV version were significantly higher than those reported by Boehm for the low socioeconomic groups in her sample, even though the mean differences between the normative data reported by Boehm and the results of the presentation of the standard version of the test to children in the St. Louis sample were not significantly different.

Lexical Relativity and the Subcultural Experience

Earlier in this book, we considered some evidence regarding the Whorfian hypothesis for wholistic cultural contrasts. In this section we shall suggest a related phenomenon for subcultural contrasts. To do this we shall rely heavily on an interesting report by Dawis, Soriano, Siojo, and Haynes (1974) of the University of Minnesota. They dealt with words that are common to both dialects but have different underlying meanings that yield differences in evaluating functional relations among word pairs.

The nonwhite subject group which Dawis et al. studied consists of several minority groups (black Americans, 25.93 percent; Mexican Americans, 0.26 percent; American Indians, 0.64 percent; Oriental Americans, 0.55 percent; other, 0.67 percent). (The remaining 71.15 percent of the subjects were white.)[1] We shall focus on differences between white and nonwhite groups that represent extreme differences in responding (close to 0 percent or 100 percent of the nonwhite group will be attended to) so that by implication we can conclude that all or none of the black subjects affirmed or denied the functional relationships they were asked to evaluate for a given word pair.

First Source of Racial Differences in Evaluating Word Pairs

There is a significant tendency for the nonwhite group of subjects to respond positively in evaluating the presence of a particular relationship for any given word pair. These data are given in Table 10.

Reflecting on these data we note that there is a significant response tendency for a nonwhite subject to say

[1] Dawis et al. examined 3,486 subjects. Some demographic variables of possible interest for this sample are as follows:

1. All subjects were from Memphis, Tennessee.
2. They were selected from grades 10–12.
3. Six schools were represented in the sample.
4. Sex was equally represented.
5. Their ages ranged from 15 to 27, with the bulk between 15 and 17.
6. The subjects ranged over the entire SES spectrum.
7. Racial characteristics have already been given.

TABLE 10

Response bias in evaluating word pair relations

Word pair[a] relations	Number of times nonwhites have a higher percentage "yes" than whites	Total number of pairs	Percentage	Sign. test (p)
Class/ Membership	46	77	59	.125 1-tail
Activity/Use	42	52	81	.005
Functional	50	52	98	.005
Similarity/ Equivalence	57	77	74	.005
Conversion/ Process	76	85	89	.005
Order/Time	23	32	72	.025
Opposite	25	29	89	.005
Cause/Effect	55	64	86	.005
Pattern	21	21	100	.005
Association	34	53	64	.050
Total	429	542	79	

[a]Definitions: (1) *Class/Membership*: Two words have this relation when one thing includes the other, or when one thing is included in the other. (2) *Activity/Use*: Two words have this relation when both words name things that perform the same activity or have the same use. (3) *Functional*: Two words have this relation when one word names an object that performs some activity on or for the other. (4) *Similarity/Equivalence*: Two words have this relation when both name things that are similar or equivalent. (5) *Conversion/Process*: Two words have this relation when one word names a thing that is made (converted or processed) from the other. (6) *Order/Time*: Two words have this relation when one thing follows the other in a certain order or in time, or when one thing is followed by the other. (7) *Opposite*: Two words have this relation when one is the opposite of the other. (8) *Cause/Effect*: Two words have this relation when one causes (brings about) the other or is caused by the other. (9) *Pattern*: Two words have this relation when one word has a pattern like the other; for example, one word sounds like the other, or rhymes with the other, or is the other word spelled backwards. (10) *Association*: Two words have this relation when they are often used or thought of as going together.

"yes" regardless of which word pair is presented, with the exception of Class/Membership. Ideally, this response bias should be corrected for before further analyses are conducted on these data, but for our present purposes we need not do this. It may be useful to speculate that most of the relations producing a significant difference have to do with dynamic changes, or dynamic uses of the words (e.g., Conversion/Process; Order/Time; Cause/Effect; Activity/Use) and function. All implicate transformational changes, or pragmatic uses with respect to the subculture one comes from.

Second Source of Racial Differences
in Evaluating Word Pairs

Our purpose is to speculate on the possible source of difference obtained for particular word pairs as a function of white versus nonwhite group membership. Table 11 shows some particular examples that will stimulate our speculations.

One striking difference we believe is clearly tied to the subcultural experience in these data is the relationship of *Bible* to *Read*. We see under the relation Class/Membership that 92 percent of the nonwhites (by implication this is the majority of blacks) have affirmed that *Bible* and *Read* stand in a Class/Membership relation. Only 39 percent of the whites affirm this. How might we account for this difference? Until recently the majority of blacks have come from rural poor environments. In this milieu, the Bible was the chief reading material. The whites, on the other hand, most likely had a wider reading range and for this reason were reluctant to implicate a Class/Membership relationship between *Bible* and *Read*. Thus, if we are correct, this example of lexical difference is clearly tied to the ethnography of subcultural experience and its historical roots.

Another example of this is the relationship between *Plow* and *Mule*. Again 93 percent of the nonwhites affirm

TABLE 11

Some lexical examples

Relation	Word pair	Percent yes	
		White	Nonwhite
Class/Membership	Gale:Sail	56	0
	Slide:Steep	28	0
	Press:Woman	57	93
	Water:Drink	57	93
	Window:Light	37	0
	Dream:Night	40	7
	Bible:Read	39	92
	Sickness:Dying	50	92
	Fruit:Ripe	50	92
Activity/Use	Wool:Sheep	68	100
	Plow:Mule	55	93
	Garage:Car	45	93
	Arm:Elbow	55	93
	Track:Road	65	100
	Shovel:Clear	37	0
Functional	Moss:Rock	57	6
	Street:Address	21	90
	Sheep:Farmer	42	90
	Child:Family	58	100
	Tobacco:Field	39	90
Similarity/Equivalence	Olive:Pit	48	0
	School:Military	41	0
	Miss:Lass	52	6
Conversion/Process	Sickness:Cold	44	92
	Foot:Walk	38	100
	Sleep:Night	27	100
	High:Tall	31	100

Note. From "Demographic factors in the education of relations in analogy word pairs" by R. V. Dawis, L. V. Soriano, L. R. Siojo, and J. Haynes (Technical Report No. 3). University of Minnesota, Department of Psychology, 1974. Used with permission.

TABLE 11

Some lexical examples (*continued*)

Relation	Word pair	Percent yes White	Percent yes Nonwhite
	Yellow:Sun	27	92
	Bath:Wash	50	100
	Hammer:Tool	31	100
	Eating:Ate	65	100
Order/Time	Earth:Sun	33	94
	Summer:Winter	57	94
	Swift:River	46	0
Cause/Effect	Begin:End	61	100
	Issue:Mint	32	0
	Gale:Sail	32	0
	Bible:Holy	46	100
	Blue:Cold	54	100
Association	Birth:Death	55	100
	Red:White	55	100
	Moon:Earth	62	100
	Square:Carpenter	42	0

Class/Membership while only 55 percent of the whites did. The poor black farmer in the South probably had recourse more often to animal-drawn plows than did the whites, whom we speculate may have had more frequent experience with machine-driven equipment. We realize of course that not all the examples given lend themselves to this rural-urban explanation. Some of the differences are undoubtedly due to momentary misconstruing of the intended relationship. Thus, Class/Membership may have been momentarily confused with one of the other relations, for example, *Child* related to *Family*. We fail to see how 100 percent of the nonwhites could affirm this as a functional relationship unless they were confusing it momentarily as a Class/Membership one. The whites are equally guilty of such putative confusion—for example, *Olive* related to *Pit*. As an equivalence relationship, 48 percent of the whites affirmed this but there are cherry pits, plum pits, etc. We fail to see that olive is necessarily equivalent to pit. The whites seem to have confused equivalence with Class/Membership.

While Dawis et al. plan to study lexical difference as it pertains to solving word analogy problems, we have chosen to speculate on these differences as evidence of Whorfian relativity at the subcultural level. The differences are clearly there and perhaps can best be understood only by returning to the speech communities which gave birth to these differences. Thus, we wish to underscore once again the cruciality of ethnographic exploration in formulating a theory of subcultural differences.

Summary

Apparent vocabulary differences between black and white children were found in some cases to disappear when lower-class black children were tested using BEV as the medium of interchange between child and examiner. This suggests that some aspects of vocabulary difference are attributable to relative unfamiliarity with the SE language system in which tests are traditionally administered. Thus, unfamiliarity with the syntactic code used to conduct the interview obscured the true level of knowledge of SE vocabulary.

Reviews on semantic relationships underlying pairs of words suggest that some true differences may exist between the lexicons of black Americans and white Americans. The study did not use words that were uniquely known to black Americans but used instead words of everyday occurrence to most individuals.

Both results again point to the clarifying influence of the effect of embedded subcultural experience on cognitive functioning as mediated by different language codes.

FUNCTION

Function in Naturalistic Settings

Although the data regarding subcultural differences in language function are somewhat scant, there are some representative studies of differing degrees of robustness that are worth discussing (see Cook-Gumperz, 1973; Freedle & Hall, 1973; Hall & Freedle, 1973; Horner, 1968; Ward, 1971).

Using the theory of social control and language use developed by Bernstein (1971) as a framework, Cook-Gumperz (1973) examined social-class differences in terms of the mother's practices of social control, that is, the emphasis the mother placed on the use of language in the control of her child. She viewed the mother's practices in terms of, for example, the concepts of *positional* and *personal* control.

The definition of these two modes of control revolves around one's orientation to status. Personal control orients the child toward understanding his own personal needs, while positional control orients the child toward submitting to the commands of others simply because they hold a dominant social position with respect to the child's. For example, suppose the child asks to stay up late to watch a special movie on television. A mother using a personal control mode might say, "I don't think you should, because if you do you're going to be too tired to get up for school in the morning." A positional control mode might be, "You do as *I* say; now go to bed!"

Focusing on the mother, the author asked essentially the following questions:

1. Are there social class differences in modes of control?
2. Is the working class more likely than the other classes to use positional forms of control and the middle class to use personal forms of control?

She also examined the child's perception of social control in the same terms.

With respect to language, Cook-Gumperz analyzed the mother's language and communication styles in terms of Bernstein's theory of language code, i.e., the presence of elaborated and restricted codes. A major question in her research was, "What is the relationship between the mother's style of social control and her language code?" She hypothesized that there would be a strong relationship between the use of an elaborated code and the use of personal social control, and also between the use of a restricted code and that of positional control. Finally, she considered the consequences of the mother's control for the child's cognitive development.

Using an interview schedule composed of both closed- and open-ended items (hypothetical situations), Cook-Gumperz explored the way in which mothers prepare their children for entering school, the mother's orientation to language, and the language used by the mother to explain things to her child.

By and large, the predictions regarding the preferred control system in Cook-Gumperz's work were borne out. In general, middle-class mothers took up strategies within the personal mode of social control; the mixed-class mothers, within the positional mode; and the working-class mothers, within the imperative mode. The data also revealed more flexibility in the use of strategies by the middle class than in the mixed or working classes.

The findings for the children's language usage were full of surprises. A positional-imperative control mode was used by all social-class groups, and the children had a smaller range of strategies than did adults. There were, however, three noticeable social-class differences: the middle-class children gave more strategies in the personal control mode; the mixed-class parents used more indirect punishment; the working-class parents used more physical punishment and an imperative strategy of control. The particular strategy chosen is undoubtedly influenced by the situation. An analysis of sex differences suggests that middle-class mothers are more likely to reason with boys than with girls, and the working-class mothers are more likely to use emotional control and reparation with girls than with boys.

With regard to the speech codes employed by the mother, the expected association between the two codes, elaborated and restricted, and the mothers' social class was borne out. The middle-class mothers tended more often to use an elaborated code and the working-class mothers a restricted code. Moreover, the two codes generally showed a clearly defined pattern of association with the control strategies. Elaborated code indicators correlated with items of verbally mediated personal control and single reasoning positional control, while restricted code indicators were associated with affective personal controls and positional rationales. Imperative controls, such as physical punishment, did not correlate with code indicators at all.

Perhaps the most interesting finding from Cook-Gumperz's work has to do with the consequences for the child of the mother's preferred method of social control as well as her speech code. Cook-Gumperz investigated the relationship between these two aspects of the mother's behavior and the child's verbal test score. She found that the mother's control system influences verbal test scores and that positional control through a restricted code appears to depress these scores.

Cook-Gumperz thus found a pattern of social-class differences in the mothers' presentation of social rules to their children. The class differences are transmitted to children through class-related parental perceptions of control relations, and the differences influence the child's cognitive development, as revealed through verbal IQ test scores. These class-related associations, moreover, occur both between and within classes. Interestingly, one might argue that habitual uses of certain language styles affect cognitive functioning, which would appear to qualify as a modified Whorfian viewpoint concerning language and thought. If so, we again see how the Whorfian hypothesis may operate at subcultural levels that tend to use certain control modes more than others.

Earlier in this book, we highlighted the differences between the wholistic culture and the embedded subculture groups. Inasmuch as the Cook-Gumperz work contrasts socioeconomic levels in a somewhat homogeneous culture in Britain, we are faced with the following question, Can the socioeconomic levels in Britain be characterized as embedded subcultural experiences?

We believe that there is an essential difference between black experience in the United States and the experience of lower-class whites in Britain. We reiterate some of the important points made earlier—historically, blacks in the United States were embedded in a culture against their will; and they came from highly different cultural groups in terms of diversity among themselves and vis-à-vis the white majority. They were disenfranchised politically, and they were hampered educationally insofar as they were forbidden to read. We believe that these characteristics constitute the embedded subcultural experience and that this experience is distinct from that associated with social stratification within a wholistic culture. Even though Cook-Gumperz's work extends to racial contrasts, more empirical work must be done before the contrast is fully established. Some tentative results in this regard have been reported by Horner (1968) and Ward (1971).

In a pioneer effort, Horner (1968) sought to penetrate the mystery of the black lower-class urban home in the United States and attempted to replace speculation with facts about the nature and frequency of verbal behavior in the world of the poor child. To this end, she monitored the verbal world of two 3-year-old black children, a boy and a girl. Each child was electronically monitored for two days, a weekday and a weekend day, in and around the home. As a result of this process, the child's network of verbal inter-action was determined along with the frequency of inter-action with various groups and individuals in the environment. Moreover, context variables, including locales and activities co-occurring with verbal behavior, and audience variables were examined. Using Skinner's operant framework, an analysis of the functions of verbal behavior for the child and his interlocutors was conducted.

A similar piece of work in the ethnography of communication has been done by Ward (1971). Ward went beyond Horner and investigated an entire community and its communicative habits as a whole. In essence, Ward was concerned about two questions:

1. What are the boundaries of the speech community?
2. How do the people observed define and carry out situations requiring communication?

To answer these questions, Ward focused on concepts and situations which the community felt to be true to life, using child-rearing practices as the point of departure.

Ward made intensive observations of children in some homes outside New Orleans, Louisiana. Her starting point was the activities of seven families, for the purpose of assessing the boundary of their experience. Her preconception was that knowledge of a child's patterns of experiential limits was a map of her or his conceptual limits. Ward was also seeking information about the child's linguistic contacts, specifically, to whom he talked, who talked to him, what they talked about, and under what circumstances he used language or needed to respond to others—in short, what his language diet was.

Ward's findings are as provocative as they are important.

1. In less than 5 percent of the total utterances recorded, reciprocal expansions were clearly operative in either the child's or the parents' speech.
2. Conversations between adults and children were characterized by little reciprocity.
3. Talk for the sake of talk between adults and children was not the mode.
4. Mothers did not imitate or expand the speech of children to any extent; however, they did expand their own speech to children.
5. Expansions of sentences was not the usual manner in which adults addressed other adults and mature teen-agers.
6. Adult speech was characterized by false starts, that is, communication-securing devices such as *you know*, and the use of multisyllabic lexical items.
7. The mean sentence length for adult–adult speech was 15.5 words per sentence.

8. Corrections of child language always centered around the standard of behavior and not around the standard of language.

9. Children actively engaged in seeking information were treated, not as being inquiring and curious, but rather as noisy and demanding.

10. Mothers did not feel a very heavy responsibility toward language instruction.

11. Children were not expected to exhibit any range of manners, skills, or special knowledge, i.e., talents which could be demonstrated for the benefit of admiring friends and relatives. They were responsible only for taking care of themselves and for following orders.

12. It is the special province of older children to impart the type of knowledge that requires drill.

13. There is almost no subject matter initiated by children that adults feel it incumbent upon them to pursue.

14. Adults select the topic of conversation.

15. Most of what adults and parents say to children is administrative speech.

16. The families in question can perhaps best be characterized as positional- rather than person-oriented.

17. Imperatives are the primary form of verbal manipulation.

18. Outside of administrative speech and imperatives, questions are the most frequent interchange. Most of the questions originate with adults.

19. Parents are not in the habit of asking questions to which they already know the answer.

20. The style of language used can perhaps best be called apodictic.

21. Parents frequently engage in reciprocal aggressive physical acts with children.

22. Children acquire a restricted language code.
23. The years from 1 or 2 to 6, the most crucial ages for learning language, are the period of best adult contacts and stimulation for these children.
24. The children are at their best in peer groups.

Ward's work represents the kind of ethnography that is necessary if we are to get a firm handle on the nature of the black American's unique system of language and its impact on other salient aspects of the black life-style. One of her most relevant findings for the educational enterprise is that in the community where her work was done, children are to be seen and not heard. Adults never engage in conversation with children for the sake of conversation. The educational enterprise must become sensitive to such ethnographic facts in seeking to educate children from nonmainstream backgrounds.

Function in Experimental Settings

To date, most of the experiments that touch upon language function have been conducted in controlled experimental settings. These studies vary enormously in the degree to which they are sensitive to ethnographic function. We shall touch on a few of the more relevant ones.

Williams and Naremore (1969) elicited sentences in home interviews with 40 fifth- and sixth-grade children from low- and middle- to high-income backgrounds. Both black and white children were studied. They found that socioeconomic status and the topic of the discussion were more significant factors in the proportion of usage of elaborated structures than was race, with low-income black children using the structures less frequently than low-income white children.

Heider, Cazden, and Brown (1968) examined the ability of low-income white and black children and middle-income white children to encode the properties of abstract figures taken from Krauss and Glucksberg (1967). They also studied faces as stimuli. The analysis focused on the number of wholistic descriptions versus the number of part descriptions, which encompassed only a piece of the total picture. On the production end of the task, the white middle class differed significantly from the white and black lower classes. The white middle class produced fewer wholistic descriptions than did the two lower-class groups. On the comprehension side of the task, the descriptions produced by these three groups were presented to the same groups for identification of the correct target picture. White middle-class subjects were best able to use analytic part descriptions in identifying the correct picture. What is interesting is that the white lower-class and black lower-class groups also performed better when given the analytic description. This presents a puzzle, inasmuch as it raises the question of why these lower-class children should, on the productive end, prefer emitting wholistic descriptions but clearly make more effective use of the part descriptions. There appears to be a mismatch between productive and comprehension functions.

With regard to the subcultural experience, the data from the sentence imitation experiment done by Hall and Freedle (1973) has implications for the question of how language functions in a controlled setting.

To interpret the patterns shown in Figure 1, it will be useful to recall an interpretation by Baratz (1969). She maintains that the SE and BEV dialects are different *coding schemes*. We take this to mean that an individual who is more familiar with BEV, as was observed for the lower-class blacks in these data, will tend to encode, in his short-term semantic memory, sentence information corresponding to the BEV

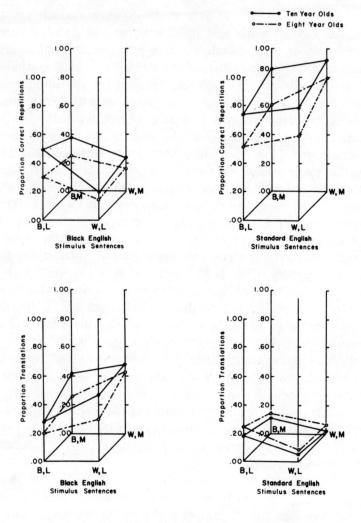

FIGURE 1

The proportion of correct repetitions and translations
over all grammatical forms for standard English
and black English vernacular.

code. Correspondingly, a person who is more familiar with SE, as observed in white middle-class subjects in these data, will tend to encode, in his short-term semantic memory, sentence information corresponding to the SE code.

This approach can be applied to the data shown in Figure 1 and Table 12 in the following way. If the incoming stimulus for a black lower-class subject is in his familiar dialect, he does not have to do any extra work in encoding the information, since it is already in the preferred dialect. His short-term semantic memory is, in effect, in a BEV state. If he retrieves the information in the same form in which it is coded in his memory, he will get a larger number of BEV structures correct in a large percentage of cases. The same black subject also receives SE sentences but he would tend to encode many of these in BEV form. When it is time to retrieve them, he would, in turn, give back many "translations," since by assumption he tends to retrieve information in terms of the representation in his semantic memory.

Exactly the reverse argument holds for the middle-class white subjects. They should get a large proportion of standard structures correct and also tend to give a large proportion of translations from BEV into SE. A reflection on the data portrayed in Figure 1 will show that this is exactly what happens. Middle-class blacks and lower-class whites fall somewhere in between these two extremes. Presumably this means that they have no clearcut dialect preference, perhaps because they are equally familiar with both SE and BEV forms. The regularity of these results holds for both 8- and 10-year-olds.

The Freedle-Hall Information-processing Model

While some of the preceding material has been reported by Baratz (1969), Hall and Freedle (1973) have extended her coding idea in an information-processing sense. We shall now

TABLE 12

The proportion of correct repetitions (C), translations (T), and deletions (D) for grammatical forms in SE and BEV stimulus sentences as a function of race, socioeconomic status, and age

Stimulus and response types		Age 8				Age 10			
		Black lower	Black middle	White lower	White middle	Black lower	Black middle	White lower	White middle
3rd person singular									
SE	C	.350	.538	.525	.800	.654	.842	.762	.892
BEV	C	.420	.308	.129	.079	.392	.296	.158	.183
SE	T	.304	.196	.108	.071	.242	.100	.079	.029
BEV	T	.225	.333	.346	.679	.371	.204	.646	.642
SE	D	.346	.267	.367	.129	.104	.058	.158	.079
BEV	D	.354	.358	.525	.242	.238	.200	.196	.175
Copula									
SE	C	.657	.676	.652	.786	.824	.924	.786	.895
BEV	C	.200	.150	.033	.042	.242	.192	.042	.100
SE	T	.057	.024	.005	.000	.024	.000	.005	.000
BEV	T	.325	.317	.408	.492	.533	.592	.592	.750
SE	D	.286	.300	.343	.214	.152	.076	.210	.105
BEV	D	.475	.533	.558	.467	.142	.133	.367	.150

Negation									
SE	C	.400	.511	.433	.567	.600	.700	.600	.789
BEV	C	.381	.324	.210	.181	.552	.486	.252	.348
SE	T	.389	.289	.311	.300	.333	.267	.233	.167
BEV	T	.043	.052	.052	.105	.062	.110	.110	.114
SE	D	.211	.200	.256	.133	.178	.033	.167	.044
BEV	D	.576	.624	.738	.714	.386	.595	.638	.538
Use of *if*									
SE	C	.083	.233	.433	.800	.267	.467	.800	.917
BEV	C	.883	.583	.250	.083	.817	.583	.150	.100
SE	T	.750	.567	.200	.083	.683	.433	.083	.033
BEV	T	.000	.183	.350	.667	.067	.317	.700	.867
SE	D	.167	.200	.367	.117	.050	.100	.117	.050
BEV	D	.117	.233	.400	.250	.117	.100	.150	.033
Past marker									
SE	C	.753	.786	.780	.913	.780	.893	.920	.967
BEV	C	.473	.400	.193	.247	.553	.520	.293	.300
SE	T	.140	.080	.013	.013	.173	.100	.013	.000
BEV	T	.347	.320	.413	.520	.387	.393	.573	.613
SE	D	.107	.133	.207	.073	.047	.007	.067	.033
BEV	D	.180	.280	.393	.233	.060	.087	.067	.020

TABLE 12

The proportion of correct repetitions (C), translations (T), and deletions (D) for grammatical forms in SE and BEV stimulus sentences as a function of race, socioeconomic status, and age (*continued*)

Stimulus and response types		Age 8				Age 10			
		Black lower	Black middle	White lower	White middle	Black lower	Black middle	White lower	White middle
Possessive									
SE	C	.300	.467	.483	.800	.883	.783	.683	.867
BEV	C	.250	.150	.033	.050	.467	.250	.067	.183
SE	T	.250	.150	.017	.033	.300	.100	.050	.000
BEV	T	.167	.267	.283	.433	.333	.467	.383	.433
SE	D	.450	.383	.500	.167	.117	.117	.267	.133
BEV	D	.583	.583	.683	.517	.200	.283	.550	.383
Plural marker									
SE	C	.600	.633	.575	.792	.800	.858	.833	.908
SE	T	.008	.017	.000	.008	.025	.008	.008	.000
SE	D	.392	.350	.425	.200	.175	.133	.158	.092
Use of *be*									
BEV	C	.292	.183	.033	.142	.358	.317	.117	.142
BEV	T	.217	.250	.267	.317	.275	.608	.367	.308
BEV	D	.492	.567	.700	.542	.367	.075	.517	.550

analyze the information-processing idea as a model that will, among other things, help us explain the regularity between translation scores, deletion scores, and correct recall scores as a function of race, socioeconomic status, and age. The basic data for our discussion were presented in Table 12.

The cultural context of language. It will be useful to address ourselves to the cultural context of language use in order to place the information-processing formulation in proper perspective. To accomplish this, we shall rely in part on some recent work in ethnographic psychology—especially that of Cole, Gay, Glick, and Sharp (1971).

A portion of the Cole et al. empirical work suggests to us the possibility that there are at least some experimental tasks that members of different subcultures respond to in basically the same manner. By this we mean that the information-processing steps by which a particular problem is solved can be isomorphic across the various subject populations tested. One example in the Cole et al. work which leads us to this conclusion is their revision of what is called the Kendler Inference Experiment (see Kendler, Kendler, & Carrick, 1966). The abstract characterization of the experiment, not the specifics of the task, is what concerns us at the moment.

The Kendler task has two major considerations for crosscultural comparisons:

1. the familiarity of the objects which constitute the inference task
2. the degree to which a prelearned associative link has been established across the task objects

Cole et al. (1971) tested seven variants of these task features and concluded that Kpelle and American children of several ages respond in very similar fashion for many variants of the task. The result can be interpreted to mean that if a full information-processing analysis of the inference task were constructed, then the same underlying cognitive steps (decisions) would be required to explain the data of each population of subjects; the only difference, if there is any, would presumably be reflected in the magnitude of the model parameters which characterize each step of the decision process.

If the task happens to emphasize aspects of the culture that are unique to that culture, then it may be necessary to postulate cognitive decisions that differ across the populations tested. If, however, the task has been carefully constructed so as to tap cognitive decisions that are universal to all cultures, then the cognitive decision parameters may well be statistically identical across populations.

Finally, there may be tasks which favor a mixture of these two basic types, for example, a task in which some of the steps favor unique cultural knowledge and the others cut across the universal features of all cultures. In terms of guideline principles, a critical feature of these comparisons may involve the similarity of one culture to another with respect to the functional equivalences to which language is put.

The model. Although many hypotheses could be tested, we shall present only one. Let us assume that the subcultures of the same wholistic culture, such as one finds in the United States, are so similar that every statistic on which the subgroups are compared may be isomorphic in their basic underlying information-processing steps.

This is the assumption we shall act upon in discussing the sentence-recall data we mentioned earlier. The model to be presented in this discussion is taken from a report by Freedle and Hall (1973).

The task they modeled was presented to 240 subjects. The sample consisted of 8- and 10-year-olds, with an equal number of blacks and whites, males and females, and lower- and middle-socioeconomic levels. The members of each of the samples were considered to be members of highly similar subcultures in contemporary urban United States. Each group responded to sentences presented in either SE or BEV.

We will consider first what a subject must do in responding to this task. On any one trial, he is to read a sentence that either matches or mismatches his preferred dialect. If it matches his preferred dialect, we assume that this may influence his ability to code the semantic and syntactic information in his short-term memory; also, it may affect the accuracy with which he can retrieve the information when he starts his overt recall of the sentence. Each one of these three aspects (preference, coding in memory, and retrieval) can be considered as steps in an information-processing model. A full elaboration of this model would help to account for errors and deletions that are made in the task by introducing steps in the process that reflect, for example, failure to store information in short-term memory and/or failure to retrieve the information stored in memory.

Notice that some of the facts that affect the covert information-processing decisions may be identified as cognitive ability parameters such as memory; other factors may be more appropriately characterized as being identified with qualities unique to the subcultures tested, namely, preference for using one dialect over another. Thus, the latter factor of the decision model, which measures degree of preference for one dialect system over another, should be a function of what race and social class the experimental subject belongs to.

The sentence-recall task we have examined at this point seems to represent a mixed system, inasmuch as we can identify memory coding steps that should yield the same parameter values for the populations tested. It also involves a dialect preference step on which the various subcultures are likely to differ significantly. Clearly, finding significant differences in dialect preference cannot be construed as implying the superiority or inferiority of any subcultural group. Finding significant differences on the memory parameter would require a more careful examination of the sources of the differences. For example, if it is found that the memory parameter interacts with the type of dialect sentence with which the subject is presented, then one is not justified in pretending that the steps in the information-processing model are independent. Also, if interaction occurs, one would not be justified in concluding that one subgroup is superior to the others if its members have a significantly higher memory parameter value. Instead, one should attempt to track down the source of the interaction in terms of the task requirements as a function of the subcultural differences.

In this section we will deal with developmental changes that occur across various social groups of basically the same culture. The same information-processing model is assumed to be appropriate at both age levels (8 and 10) inasmuch as both groups share basically the same culture. Had the two age groups been widely different (say, a group of 3-year-olds contrasted with a group of 70-year-olds), one could question whether the same information-processing model were appropriate to several age groups. Again, the underlying conception of the similarity of one subpopulation to another is the source of this intuition, just as the similarity among subcultures of the same basic culture was the source of our surmise that the same information-processing model may apply to each population tested.

For the age range tested, we predicted that age differences would show up as primarily differences in magnitude of the memory parameter. Furthermore, we expected that each subpopulation would show an increase in the memory parameter as a function of increasing age (here, from age 8 to age 10). We did not make similar regularizing assumptions about how the magnitude of the dialect preference parameter would change with age for each of the subpopulations because we felt that a much more complex network of social pressures operates, causing some social groups to show a decrease in preference for a given dialect and others an increase in preference. The nature of the information-processing model that we fitted was such that we will still be able to make intelligent statements regarding changes in the magnitude of the dialect preference parameter after each set of data has been fitted.

Specifics of the model. We will outline first the specifics of the information-processing model used for a sentence-recall task using SE and BEV sentences as stimuli. Eight groups were examined separately:

> white lower-class 8-year-olds
> white lower-class 10-year-olds
> black lower-class 8-year-olds
> black lower-class 10-year-olds
> white middle-class 8-year-olds
> white middle-class 10-year-olds
> black middle-class 8-year-olds
> black middle-class 10-year-olds

In each group there were an equal number of male and female subjects. Every subject received 30 sentences to imitate, half of which were presented in SE and half in BEV. Using a scoring scheme given in greater detail by Hall and Freedle (1973), we obtained the proportions of correct imitations, of deletions and/or substitutions, as well as translation responses for each of the following 14 grammatical structures:

SE	BEV
third-person singular	third-person singular
copula	copula
negation	negation
use of the conditional *if* clause	use of the *if* conditional
past marker	past marker
possessive	possessive
use of plural nouns	use of the *be* construction

Examples of these were given in Table 2.

As already mentioned, several things can occur in response to a particular structure. The subject may repeat it correctly, translate it into a form appropriate to the other dialect, fail to respond, and/or use some novel response in place of the correct one. Deletions and novel responses were scored together. The information-processing model is intended to account for all the patterns of correct repetitions, deletions, and translations that occur for each grammatical structure within and across dialects for each of the eight groups of subjects.

The information-processing model is clarified in Figure 2. Each branch of the model is labeled by a Roman numeral to facilitate reference to each branch of the tree structure.

At the top of the diagram is the presentation of a particular stimulus sentence. Whether the sentence is in SE or BEV is not significant at this point because the same abstract model is used for both types of structures. Once the stimulus sentence is received, the subject either comprehends it (I) or fails to comprehend it (II). Since all the subjects with whom

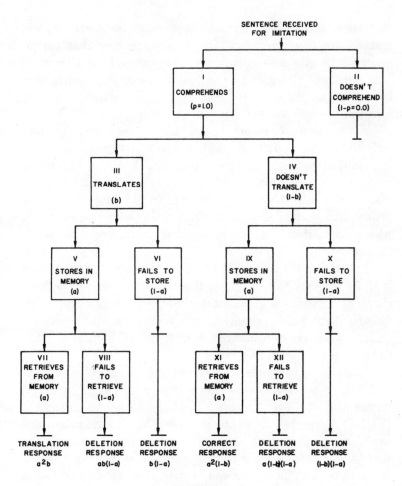

FIGURE 2

Information-processing assumptions for a sentence imitation task in two dialects. (From "An information-processing approach to some problems in developmental sociolinguistics" by R. Freedle and W. S. Hall. Paper presented at the biennial meeting of the International Society for the Study of Behavioral Development, University of Michigan, Ann Arbor, August 1973.)

we dealt in this experiment were older subjects, it will greatly simplify our model if we assume here that for all intents and purposes all subjects comprehend the import of each sentence presented them, even though we realize that the white middle-class subjects may find some of the BEV sentences to be strange.

After comprehension, either the subject will translate (III) the sentence into the dialect opposite the one in which the simulus sentence was presented (the degree to which this is done will be a function of his preference for coding in one dialect over the other) or he will fail to translate it (IV). The probability that he will translate is given by the parameter b, which can thus be interpreted as a dialect preference parameter.

Below Roman numerals III and IV we see that the model is quite similar. For example, the subject either successfully stores the results of the prior decision (III) in memory (V) or fails to store it (VI); similarly, below decision IV, the subject either will store the outcome of decision IV in memory (IX) or will fail to store it (X).

If the subject stores the information successfully at V, he will either successfully retrieve this information when it comes time to overtly recall it (VII) or fail to retrieve it (VIII). When he fails to retrieve the information, the assumption will be that the result is a deletion response. Also if the subject fails to store the information at VI, this too will contribute to the observed magnitude of the deletion response. Below branch IX we see the same kind of structure: either the subject retrieves the information in the form that he stored it in (XI) or he fails to do so (XII). Failure to do so again contributes to the magnitude of the deletion response, as does failure to store the information at step X.

In sum, there are four pathways of the decision tree which contribute to a deletion response, each of which has a different probability of occurring, as we can see below branches VIII, VI, XII, and X. The probability $ab(1-a)$ is obtained by multiplying the parameter estimates encountered from the top of the figure down to branch VIII. At branch I is the value 1.0; this is multiplied by parameter b, which occurs at branch III; this in turn is multiplied by parameter a, which occurs at branch V; and finally parameter $(1-a)$, which occurs at branch VIII, is multiplied by all the above. The net result is $ab(1-a)$.

A correct response has probability $a^2(1-b)$ of occurring, as Figure 2 illustrates. A translation response has probability $a^2 b$ of occurring; finally, a deletion response has an overall probability of $1-a^2$ of occurring. All three of these probabilities sum to 1.0.

The unrestricted model. The unrestricted model refers to the a and b parameters estimated for each age group. (Later we will present a restricted model, which makes a linearity assumption about how the magnitude of the memory parameter a changes from age 8 to age 10. The reason for the restricted model is to gain degrees of freedom for fitting the model to the data in a nontrivial way; the unrestricted model exhausts all the degrees of freedom and, in so doing, achieves a perfect fit to the data.)

We shall now use the parameter values from the unrestricted model to compare the several subcultural groups to determine possible significant differences in some or all the parameters. The parameter values are presented in Table 13.

Memory: Parameter a comparisons. When age is ignored, middle-class blacks are equal to middle-class whites in memory for SE sentences ($p = .395$, 1-tailed, n.s.). Also, middle-class blacks are not different from middle-class whites in memory for BEV sentences ($p = .212$, 1-tailed, n.s.).

TABLE 13

Estimates of translation (*b*) and memory (*a*) parameters from the unrestricted information-processing model

Subject group	Grammatical structure	8-year-olds		10-year-olds	
		Translation parameter (*b*)	Memory parameter (*a*)	Translation parameter (*b*)	Memory parameter (*a*)
Black lower class	SE				
	Third	465	809	270 (237)	948 (889)
	Copula	080	845	028 (017)	921 (910)
	Negation	493	888	191 (233)	870 (935)
	If	900	913	719 (731)	945 (949)
	Past	157	945	182 (176)	976 (968)
	Possessive	455	742	357 (315)	966 (850)
	Plural	013	780	030 (000)	908 (872)
	BEV				
	Third	349	809	486 (487)	873 (885)
	Copula	619	725	720 (778)	944 (840)
	Negation	101	651	101 (114)	784 (797)
	If	000	940	076 (097)	940 (965)
	Past	423	906	412 (407)	970 (945)
	Possessive	400	646	416 (394)	894 (794)
	Be	431	714	512 (440)	796 (834)

See note at end of table, page 93.

Black middle class

SE

Third	267	856	106	(093)	971	(955)
Copula	034	837	000	(000)	961	(948)
Negation	361	894	276	(268)	983	(967)
If	709	894	481	(482)	949	(967)
Past	092	931	101	(085)	996	(978)
Possessive	243	785	113	(107)	940	(932)
Plural	026	806	009	(018)	931	(939)

BEV

Third	520	801	630	(618)	894	(937)
Copula	679	683	772	(783)	918	(900)
Negation	138	613	185	(256)	772	(878)
If	239	875	352	(356)	949	(961)
Past	444	849	430	(430)	956	(953)
Possessive	640	646	651	(637)	847	(889)
Be	577	658	657	(683)	962	(893)

White lower class

SE

Third	171	796	094	(080)	918	(902)
Copula	008	811	006	(027)	889	(909)
Negation	418	863	280	(290)	936	(934)
If	316	796	094	(060)	940	(902)
Past	016	891	014	(000)	966	(948)
Possessive	034	707	068	(072)	856	(860)
Plural	000	758	010	(000)	918	(884)

TABLE 13

Estimates of translation (b) and memory (a) parameters from the unrestricted information-processing model (continued)

Subject group	Grammatical structure	8-year-olds		10-year-olds	
		Translation parameter (b)	Memory parameter (a)	Translation parameter (b)	Memory parameter (a)
White lower class (continued)	BEV				
	Third	728	689	803 (837)	897 (851)
	Copula	925	664	934 (891)	796 (839)
	Negation	198	512	304 (379)	602 (766)
	If	583	775	824 (845)	922 (892)
	Past	682	779	664 (680)	936 (894)
	Possessive	896	562	851 (750)	671 (795)
	Be	890	548	242 (296)	695 (783)
White middle class	SE				
	Third	082	933	031 (037)	960 (965)
	Copula	000	887	000 (000)	946 (941)
	Negation	346	931	175 (165)	978 (964)
	If	094	940	035 (029)	975 (969)
	Past	014	963	000 (000)	983 (981)
	Possessive	040	913	000 (024)	931 (954)
	Plural	010	894	000 (000)	953 (944)

BEV

Third	896	871	778 (764)	908 (932)
Copula	921	730	882 (942)	922 (858)
Negation	367	535	247 (295)	680 (756)
If	889	866	897 (943)	983 (930)
Past	678	876	676 (687)	963 (935)
Possessive	896	695	703 (677)	785 (840)
Be	691	677	684 (620)	671 (831)

Note. The values in parentheses following parameters a and b for the 10-year-old data are the magnitudes estimated using the 8-year-old data from a linearity assumption regarding the hypothesized relation between the magnitude of the paramter a obtained at age 8 and the value of the same parameter a obtained at age 10. The postulated relation was of the form $a_{i,10} = a_{i,8} + d(1 - q_{i,8})$ where $a_{i,10}$ stands for the observed value of a obtained from the unrestricted model at age 10 for a particular grammatical structure i, and $a_{i,8}$ stands for the observed value of the a parameter obtained at age 8 for the same grammatical structure i. The average d value obtained for each of four groups (black, lower; black, middle; white, lower; and white, middle) was .4187, .6859, .5208, and .4754, respectively. These average d values were obtained by averaging over all 14 grammatical structures. By applying this average d value for a given group of subjects, the a values were reestimated under the restrictive assumptions about the relation of the a parameter over these two age groups; this value appears in parentheses. With each new a parameter thus estimated, it was possible to recompute a b value by employing the following equation:

$$b = \frac{a^2 + (\text{observed proportion translations}) - (\text{observed proportion corrects})}{2a^2}$$

These reestimated b values under the restrictive assumptions on the a parameter over ages 8 to 10 are also given in parentheses. The purpose of introducing this linearity assumption over age (for the a parameter over all 14 grammatical forms) was to gain degrees of freedom.

93

Again, if age is disregarded, the black lower class equals the white lower class in memory for SE sentences ($p = .092$, 2-tailed, n.s.). However, the black lower class is significantly higher in memory parameters than the white lower class when BEV sentences are examined ($p = .002$, 2-tailed).

Still, ignoring the age factor and comparing the effects of socioeconomic status within each racial group, we find that black middle-class subjects do better, but not significantly so, than do black lower-class subjects on SE sentences ($p = .090$, 1-tailed). Lower-class blacks do significantly better than middle-class blacks do on BEV sentences ($p = .046$, 1-tailed). This result is easy to understand if we remember that lower-class blacks probably speak BEV on more occasions than do middle-class blacks. This factor could also presumably explain why middle-class blacks do somewhat better (but not significantly so) on SE sentences.

Middle-class whites do significantly better than lower-class whites do in memory for SE sentences ($p = .001$, 1-tailed). However, less easy to understand is that middle-class whites also do significantly better than lower-class whites do on the BEV structures ($p = .001$, 1-tailed).

Every group improves significantly in the memory parameter when 8-year-olds are contrasted with the same parameter at age 10. This is true for BEV as well as for SE structures.

For each of the eight subject groups, there is significantly better performance on SE structures than on BEV. This particular result is important because it signifies that the ability to store and retrieve information is not independent of the dialect code in which it is presented by the experimenter. The surprise in this is that the black subjects found it easier to store and retrieve—at the level of the memory parameter only. (The reader is cautioned here that we are talking, not about proportion of correct repetitions, but about the magnitude of the underlying memory-ability parameter a.) That blacks found it easier to store and retrieve is perhaps more readily understandable if we recall from the Hall and Freedle (1973) study that in a communication task, these same blacks spontaneously produced more SE forms than BEV forms. Since our 8- and 10-year-old black subjects in the imitation study appeared to use predominantly SE dialect (at least in the setting—a school—in which we tested them) it is explicable why the same subjects found it easier to store and retrieve SE grammatical forms better than BEV forms—because they use the SE forms to a greater extent in their spontaneous speech. Consequently, what appears at first to be a counterintuitive result with the memory parameter for these black subjects can be partially interpreted with the aid of data obtained from other experimental settings—in particular, a communication study. This points up the need for one who is attempting to interpret dialect usage from a psychological modeling point of view to have data on the same subjects in a variety of different settings and tasks.

Dialect preference: Translation parameter b comparisons. The 8- and 10-year-old middle-class blacks showed a significantly greater tendency to translate from SE to BEV than did 8- and 10-year-old middle-class whites ($p < .001$, 2-tailed). This is somewhat interesting, for these same black subjects were equal to the whites with respect to the memory parameter, as we have already noted. Hence, in some cases, perhaps a dialect preference difference need not alter or interact with memory ability.

On the other hand, 8- and 10-year-old middle-class whites showed a significantly greater tendency to translate BEV into SE forms ($p < .001$, 2-tailed) than do middle-class blacks. This is hardly surprising inasmuch as the white subjects are doubtlessly quite unfamiliar with the syntax of BEV grammatical forms.

In comparison with 8- and 10-year-old white lower-class children, 8- and 10-year-old black lower-class children showed a significantly stronger preference (parameter b) for coding in BEV dialect when BEV stimuli were presented. When SE sentences were presented, black lower-class children again showed a significantly greater tendency to code in BEV than did white lower-class children ($p < .001$, 1-tailed). Both these findings are consistent with common sense: the black children learn BEV first and speak this dialect more frequently than do white children; because of this, one should expect a dialect to be stronger for them (in a preferential sense) than it is for whites of the same social class.

The restricted model. The unrestricted information-processing model presented here exhausted all the degrees of freedom in the data. In so doing, it resulted in a perfect fit to the data. Our purpose in presenting the parameters for the overly restrictive model was to examine the relative magnitudes of the values across different samples in order to determine how the various subgroups differ and how they are similar. The unrestricted model thus served a limited but useful purpose: group comparisons in parameter magnitudes. To be scientifically interesting, though, a model should not exhaust all the degrees of freedom. One way of gaining degrees of freedom in such a model is to introduce restrictive or regularizing assumptions across the different samples in one or more of the underlying parameter values. Since age appears to be quite regular in its empirical effects for each sample, we decided to introduce our simplifying assumption at this point in the model. (The particular assumption made is described in the footnote to Table 13.) The degree to which this restricted model fits the data can be seen by examining Figure 3, which presents the observed and predicted proportion of correct repetitions, deletions, and translations for SE as well as BEV grammatical forms. Results are charted for four groups: lower-class blacks, lower-class whites, middle-class blacks, and middle-class whites. One can see readily from the graphs that the observed and predicted values cluster close to the line of perfect fit, which suggests that our assumption that memory parameter a increases linearly from age 8 to age 10 may be fairly accurate.

In fitting the model to the data and observing how well they appear to agree, one is caught midstream in the scientific enterprise of deciding whether to let the model stand in its current form or to modify it. The possibility of further modification is mentioned here because it is possible to detect a very slight deviation of observed values from predicted values when SE versus BEV structures are examined. The discrepancy, though small, has the following source: in fitting a memory parameter across the two age samples, it was assumed that the same linear increase would hold regardless of whether SE or BEV forms were being considered. Such an assumption has turned out to be erroneous, inasmuch as the memory parameter a is slightly underestimated for SE forms and slightly overestimated for BEV forms. (The discrepancy can be seen in the two rightmost columns of Table 13.) The deviation could be quickly removed, of course, by fitting a different linear increase for SE and BEV forms. This has not been done here because the degree of improvement is quite negligible. In future elaborations of this information-processing model, in new experimental settings, it is possible that a more dramatic departure of observed and predicted values will be traceable

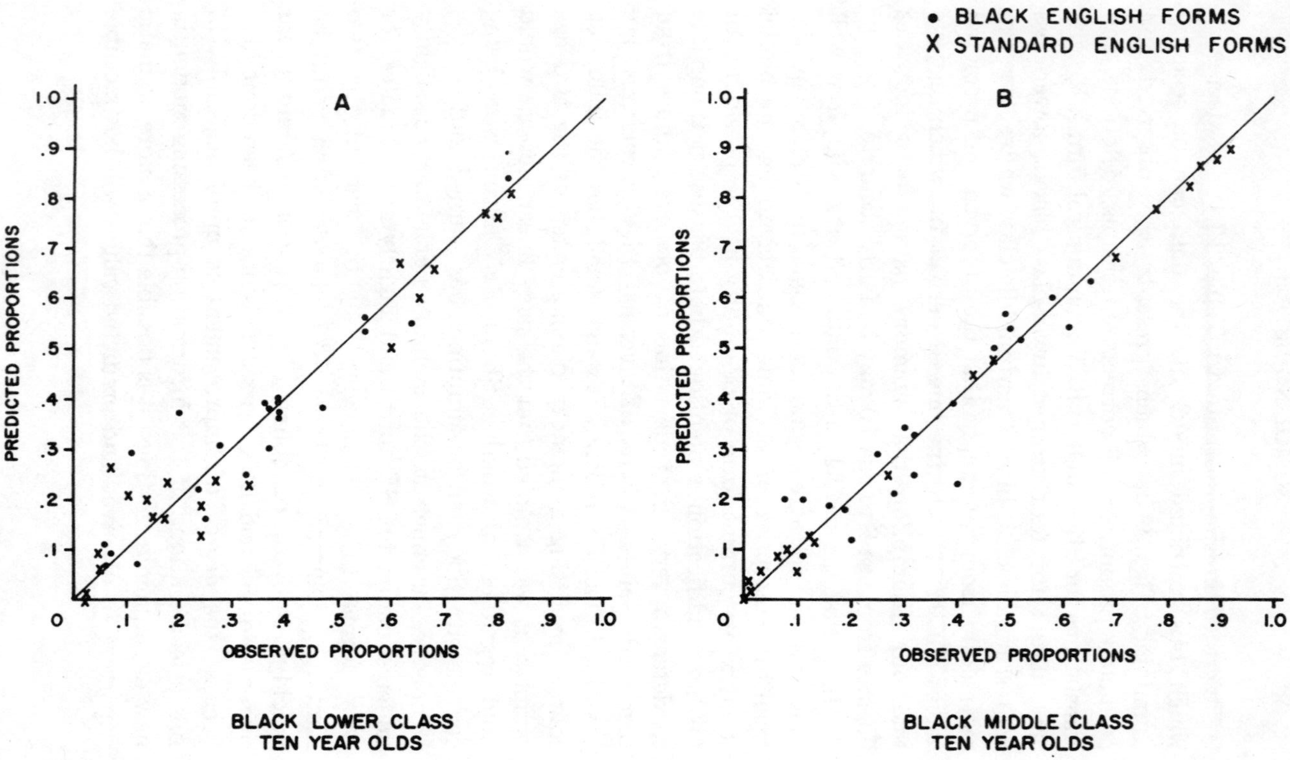

• BLACK ENGLISH FORMS
X STANDARD ENGLISH FORMS
A
B
PREDICTED PROPORTIONS
OBSERVED PROPORTIONS
0
.1
.2
.3
.4
.5
.6
.7
.8
.9
1.0
BLACK LOWER CLASS
TEN YEAR OLDS
BLACK MIDDLE CLASS
TEN YEAR OLDS

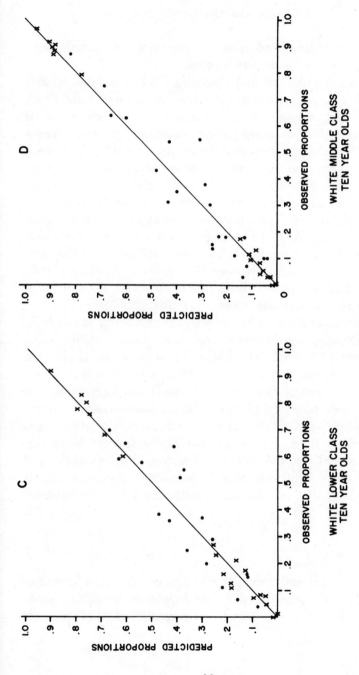

FIGURE 3

Observed and predicted proportions of correct repetitions, deletions, and translations.

to this interaction of memory parameter magnitude with dialect, but this remains to be seen.

It will be recalled that Vygotsky (1962) maintained that process changes can occur in cultural groups over time. From elementary processes more complex ones are constructed to yield voluntary memory, active attention, voluntary movement, and abstract thought. He further speculated that these complex processes become organized as functional systems subject to historical change. We wish to speculate on Vygotsky's assertions with regard to the information-processing models just presented. Our hypotheses concerning the similarity of the model for each race, socioeconomic level, and age group, which have been well fitted by the data, allow us to claim evidence for process invariance over subcultural groups over time (age of subjects). What varies in our model is not the order in which they occur but the relative magnitude with which the decisions are made. Furthermore, the model suggests a social organizational structure of such elementary processes as short-term memory, recall, and preference. This organizational structure is of a hierarchical decision method such that each subprocess has its own time and place to become operational. There are thus some similarities between our modeling efforts and Vygotsky's more general developmental theory. Moreover, with regard to the contrast between the wholistic and embedded subcultures, other information-processing models may have to be postulated and tested for data collected from other tasks.

Summary

To understand how different speech communities utilize language to carry out different functions, an ethnographic approach is required. This is true regardless of whether one is

interested in functional differences across embedded subcultures or across different socioeconomic levels within the
majority culture, or in differences that occur at more
molecular situational levels within a given speech community.
Several investigations that employed an ethnographic
approach were discussed. The British school of sociolinguists
has suggested that the social classes in Britain differ in how
language is used to control and instruct children. The uses are
found to correlate with the tendency to employ either
elaborated or restricted codes and also to correlate with IQ.
It would therefore appear that language functions can, over
time, influence cognitive functioning of the individual in an
information-processing sense.

American researchers, such as Ward (1971), have investigated an entire community and its communicative habits.
Ward's work was organized to answer two questions:

1. What are the boundaries of the speech community?
2. How do people transact situations requiring communi-
   cations?

The ethnographic investigations are of course naturalistic in
their emphasis and reveal language functions at the level of
small-group interaction as well as functions of one group with
another.

Another approach to the question of language functioning has to do with information-processing steps
(decisions) that occur within the individual when he or she
uses language.

A number of experimental approaches shed some light on
this question of intraindividual functioning for members of
embedded subcultures and members of the dominant culture.
Individuals from these two cultures were found to differ
significantly in the degree to which they described pictures in

terms of small features which occurred somewhere in the picture (e.g., "this picture has some small black spots on the bottom") as compared with wholistic descriptions (e.g., "it's the one that looks like a horse jumping over a fence"). When these same individuals had to identify pictures, the white middle-class children were best able to use the wholistic descriptions in identifying the correct picture. In contrast, the white and black lower-class children occasionally made more effective use of the part descriptions. The finding suggests that although some individuals may produce a preponderance of one type of description, when they are asked to use corresponding descriptions to choose which picture is being discussed, they only occasionally find their spontaneous predictions effective in isolating the target picture.

Another analysis of intraindividual language functions across members of subcultures revealed strong preferences for one dialect over another, depending on the class and race of the subject. Membership in one of the four subcultures studied did not, however, affect the ability to store and retrieve sentences from short-term memory.

An additional outcome of this study suggested that a greater cognitive load is carried by blacks than by whites. The greater load is a result of having more frequently to carry out a translation across dialects. Whites tended to employ only a single dialect in their responses and therefore carried out fewer translations, the cognitive load was consequently less for them in this experimental task.

INTELLECTUAL FUNCTIONING, PROBLEM SOLVING, AND CULTURE-FAIR TESTS

Kuhn (1970) has suggested that science advances when crises arise in current research paradigms. Advancement is obtained by the discovery of new paradigms which resolve the old conflict. The moribund field of IQ testing has reached a crisis level. The crisis is painfully obvious in the controversy between Jensen (1969), Jencks (1972), and Shockley (1972), on the one hand, and Kagan (1969), on the other.

We propose that by studying mental life as it relates to wholistic versus embedded cultures, a solution to this current stalemate may be forthcoming. We shall merely point the way toward an ethnographically based methodology which may eventually lead to the construction of a new paradigm.

THE CONTROVERSY OVER THE ROLE OF SUBCULTURAL EXPERIENCE IN INTELLIGENCE TEST PERFORMANCE AND PROBLEM SOLVING

The continuing controversy about the role of subcultural experience in intelligence test performance and problem solving has usually taken the form of equating subcultural experience with racial-group membership. Traditionally, on intelligence tests, vocabulary correlates more highly with all other subtests.

It is also true that the vocabulary subtests are often used as a substitute for the overall intelligence score. We have seen in the work of Williams and Rivers (1972) that the code in which the material is presented can make a dramatic difference in performance. Indeed, the performance of low-income black children matches the performance of high-income white children when this important ingredient is controlled. One must certainly conclude that part of the controversy about IQ difference and race is in some measure a function of dialect code, and in light of the Dawis, Soriano, Siojo, and Haynes (1974) report, it is also likely to be a function of true differences in vocabulary usage. Not surprisingly, given these results, we shall be critical of the literature on intelligence test performance and problem solving pertaining to the subcultural experience. The studies to be reviewed cover a wide diversity of tasks which relate to these topics.

How Culture Fair Are Intelligence Tests?

Anastasi (1965) has quite insightfully commented:

The fact that racial groups also differ in culture complicates the interpretation of observed race differences in intellectual or personality traits. Among the cultural factors that may affect performance on psychological tests are included traditions and customs, relative emphasis placed upon speed in different cultures, motivation to excel on the sort of tasks sampled by intelligence tests, and social expectancy. . . . Each culture tends to select and foster certain abilities and certain ways of behaving. Any test developed within a particular culture reflects such a selection and tends to favor individuals reared in that culture. (pp. 9–10)

Such a comment, in effect, raises the question of the culture fairness of intelligence tests and opens a possible alternative explanation, other than the often espoused genetic one, for the fifteen-point racial differential observed by many.

Jensen's Work

In contrast to Anastasi, a position which reflects great insensitivity to an ethnographic account of behavior as regards intellectual functioning can be found in the work of Jensen (1969). Perhaps we can best portray Jensen's point of view by looking at the following quotation:

> Compensatory education has been tried and it apparently has failed. Compensatory education has been practiced on a massive scale for several years in many cities across the nation. It began with auspicious enthusiasm and high hopes of educators. It had unprecedented support from Federal funds. It had theoretical sanction from social scientists espousing the major underpinning of its rationale: the "deprivation hypothesis," according to which academic lag is mainly the result of social, economic, and educational deprivation and discrimination—an hypothesis that has met with wide, uncritical acceptance in the atmosphere of society's growing concern about the plight of minority groups and the economically disadvantaged. (p. 2)

This is a rather elegant way of implying that, if people don't have the intellect, then there is little point in providing them with experiences designed to change their level of intellectual functioning. It should be noted that compensatory education programs, upon which Jensen bases his conclusions, were conducted in standard English. We have seen that this may be a critical oversight on Jensen's part because he has not taken into account the fact that many children in such programs speak either a mixed dialect or a version of black English vernacular.

Jensen postulates two types of intellectual functioning (levels I and II), which he finds useful in analyzing socioeconomic status and ethnic-group differences in intelligence. He states that level I intelligence involves "neural registration and consolidation of stimulus inputs and the formations of associations." Level II involves "self-initiated elaboration and transformation of the stimulus input before an overt response. . . ." He claims that lower-class children do as well as middle-class ones on tests measuring level I but not on those measuring level II. He further argues that heritability largely accounts for observed IQ differences. Let us now examine this hypothesis.

Inasmuch as Jensen's argument is rather tortuous, we cannot do it full justice in the pages allotted for the topic. Basically, the argument involves looking at the correlation between intelligence tests given to people who exhibit various degrees of kinship (e.g., identical twins, unrelated siblings, cousins, mother and child). If the correlation increases as a function of degree of kinship, then Jensen concludes that there is a strong heredity factor. Critical to such an argument is, of course, information on identical twins. It is critical because with no environmental difference the correlation should theoretically approach one. But twins are a relatively rare phenomenon, which necessitates gathering data over a period of years. The data used by Jensen have come from two sources: the Newman, Freeman, and Holzinger study, done in 1937 and Cyril Burt's (1955, 1957, 1958, 1959, 1961, 1963, 1966, 1968) studies done in Great Britain. Jensen views these data as supporting his thesis. (See also Burt and Howard, 1956, 1957.)

Of course it has been noted many times that the degree of genetic kinship is substantially confounded by similar environments. If blood relations are reared together, they learn a similar language, similar standards of conduct, similar modes of language communication, and similar fears and suspicions. These latter behaviors we contend are an extremely powerful influence on achieved intelligence test scores. They represent variables that would be studied in an ethnographic approach. If they are not dealt with, then one has hardly provided an adequate explanation of IQ differences. We believe that the items on IQ tests represent the perhaps unconscious bias of the members of the majority culture who generate such items.

Traditional Criticisms of Jensen

Jensen's work was immediately and sharply criticized on several points. Kagan (1969) reviewed evidence which suggested that the purported intellectual inadequacy of lower-class children may be a reflection of the style of mother-child interaction patterns. The style is such that the lower-class child is characterized as receiving less "intense exposure to maternal intervention" (p. 126). Hunt's (1969) critique centers around the idea that one must provide a rich postnatal environment in order for the inherent genetic structure to express itself and develop. He cites animal research that indicates that the brain's physical development is strongly influenced by information-processing activities.

Less critical of Jensen is Crow (1969), who has drawn attention to sampling size problems available in the studies of twins and siblings. Moreover, he questions how representative such groups are. Cronbach (1969) comments that there are many more dimensions of individual differences than are accounted for by Jensen's level I and level II distinctions in abilities.

Rather than list more of the counterarguments that have been leveled against Jensen from the viewpoint of test construction, sampling, and statistical methodology, we shall broach again the counterargument stemming from an ethnographic point of view. In particular, Cook-Gumperz's (1973) work suggests that mothers of different socioeconomic levels selectively employ the personal or the positional control mode in communication with their children, with lower-class mothers preferring the positional control. She argues that this has consequences on both the language usage and the intellectual growth of the child. This would seem to place the differences in scores on standardized tests at the level of day-to-day ethnographic functioning of a communicative type rather than at the level of genes.

Further underscoring the importance of such an interpretation has been the crosscultural ethnographic work of Cole, Gay, Glick, and Sharp (1971), who found that inference in a problem-solving task is dramatically altered by changing the familiarity of the components of the task to reflect one's cultural experience.

In addition, the work of Williams and Rivers (1972) as well as of Dawis et al. (1974) has strongly suggested to us that the subcultural experience of different minority groups produces true language differences which are not controlled for in standardized tests. When they are controlled for, many of the differences between races and socioeconomic levels should disappear, which further calls into question the purely genetic interpretation of intellectual performance. To a lesser degree, one might also argue that the critique provided by Kagan and Hunt is more compatible with an ethnographic approach insofar as they emphasize the impact of naturally occurring experiences from the environment on development.

SUBCULTURAL DIFFERENCES IN INTELLECTUAL FUNCTIONING AND PROBLEM SOLVING: THE SEARCH FOR CULTURE-FAIR TESTS

The Research

Many studies can be found that are tangentially related to the Jensen issue but have attracted less attention. They can

be broadly classified in the category of intellectual functioning and problem solving.

Bee, Van Egeren, Streissguth, Nyman, and Leckie (1969)
explored various dimensions of mother-child interactions that
may be associated with the child's cognitive development.
Using 37 males and 39 females from lower classes and 22
males and 14 females from the middle class, Bee et al.
administered a two-part experiment. The first part involved
waiting-room interaction between mother and child with
observations on verbalization and attention. The second part
was a problem-solving situation, in which mother–child
verbalization and suggestions on a toy arrangement and a
house-building problem were the focus.

The experimenters found that as compared with lower-
class mothers, middle-class mothers were less controlling and
less disapproving and gave more information and attention to
children in the waiting room. In the problem-solving situation, the middle-class pairs spent more time on the problems;
the mothers' suggestions were more numerous, less specific,
and more positive; and they also used more words, longer
sentences with greater syntactical complexity, a higher
adjective-adverb quotient, and a lower percentage of personal
pronouns than did the lower-class mothers.

Race, rather than social class, also accounted for some of
the differences in maternal behavior. Black mothers showed
lower rates of positive feedback, question-suggestion interaction, and total interaction; and the black child's rate of
information statements in the waiting room was also lower.
No major sex differences were found.

The investigators concluded that the impoverished
language environment and ineffective teaching strategies to
which the lower-class child is subjected result in a lack of the
problem-solving techniques and highly differentiated
language structure needed for a "verbally mediated analysis
of environment."

In sum, stylistic differences in language, parent-child and personal interaction, perception, and problem-solving approaches were found to influence test performance and certainly add to the difficulty of designing and interpreting culture-free tests, be they comparisons across wholistic cultures or across embedded subcultures.

Clearly there are differences among subcultures in their approach to problem solving which influence test performance. Work has of course been done to develop tests of culture and class fairness. How successful has it been?

Many of the studies reviewed in this area examined various intelligence tests—including the Peabody Picture Vocabulary Test (PPVT), the Full-Range Picture Vocabulary Test (FRPVT), the Bender-Gestalt (B-G), the Draw-a-Person (DAP) and Draw-a-Man (DAM), the Progressive Matrices (PM), and Colored Raven Progressive Matrices (CRPM)—for subcultural fairness with respect to black Americans.

Noting the class and culture bias of tests based on white norms, Coppinger and Ammons (1952) set out to evaluate the reliability and validity of the FRPVT as a measure of verbal comprehension ability and to develop norms for black children. From school records of New Orleans and Caddo Parishes, 80 black children, grades 1–8, evenly divided between sexes and urban/rural background, were chosen. After a practice session and friendly conversation with the white examiner to help ensure familiarity and rapport, the subjects were given three forms of standardized intelligence tests. Many of the items contained drawings of common activities, objects, and scenes, which the children were asked to identify.

The researchers found no consistent difference in mean scores within age levels. There were no sex or practice effects; but after age 9, there was increasing difference in urban and rural mean scores, which grew to a two-and-a-half-year rural lag by age 13. Interestingly, the urban black scores nearly equaled the rural white norm, which suggests to us that different environments make possible different abilities; and the environments selectively require the exercise of different skills, thereby leading to apparent differences in IQ. Actually, the score is more likely an indication that the subcultures of city and country life are different. Moreover, since test items are constructed by urbanites, one suspects that bias may be operating in the selection of item content. If such can be the case for rural versus urban subcultures, how much more likely may a bias enter into the selection of items that favor the majority culture as opposed to the oppressed minority cultures?

Some believe that one way to construct a culture-fair test is simply to alter the dialect in which the instructions are given and to honor the phonological requirement of the dialect in presenting each test item. But, to make only such alterations will not account for the following problem. Some nonstandard English speakers inquire about the color of the sky by asking "How be the sky?" rather than "What color is the sky?" It is clear that the distinction between these two questions can not be captured solely by phonological differences. Instead, a deeper semantic-syntactic transformation has to be applied to capture these differences. But this level of sophistication in culture-fair test construction has probably been tried only rarely. As a matter of fact, the Williams and Rivers (1972) work is a rare exemplar of this approach. Work that we think has focused on a simplistic rendering of the dialect variable on test performance is exemplified by Quay (1971, 1972, 1974).

Quay (1971, 1972, 1974), for example, attempted to evaluate the effects of several conditions—reinforcement with candy versus reinforcement with praise, and presentation of the Stanford-Binet (SB) in SE versus presentation of the SB in BEV—on 3- and 4-year-olds' performances. These evaluations showed no reliable differences or significant interactions for any of the conditions and no sex differences or examiner bias. Also, no motivational difficulties appeared to exist. The performance pattern was identical for all groups at each age level; and comprehension of the standard English SB seemed unimpaired, though the subjects spoke in dialect.

In another study, Quay (1974) provides further negative evidence with respect to the influence of dialect on test performance. Working with lower- and lower-middle-class black children in Philadelphia, Quay administered the Stanford-Binet both in its standard form and in a BEV form constructed by W. A. Stewart, a leading spokesman for the view that BEV constitutes a distinct linguistic system.

In none of the studies did Quay find support for the idea that standardized test instructions depress the performance of the black subjects, even with the rather extensive range of ages (4 to 12 years) and backgrounds explored. We suggest that these negative results may be largely a function of the formal nature of the Stanford-Binet task.

Blank and Solomon (1968) report on a one-to-one tutorial program based on the premise that substandard performances of deprived children result from the lack of a symbolic system by which to organize the plentiful stimulation around them. These researchers feel that "total enrichment" programs are destined to failure because they simply expose children to new stimuli when they need active involvement with stimuli which permit internal mental manipulation of experience. They posit four basic problems and needs.

1. A child lacks a natural firm language base for thinking and will develop one only with constant guidance.

2. There will be resistance to language acquisition by particular children, but damage can be prevented by not allowing a task to be left unfinished.

3. The short attention spans of young children necessitate relatively brief but frequent (i.e., 15 to 20 minutes per day, 5 days per week) reinforcement of new skills.

4. A new command of language will allow the child to cope more effectively with an otherwise debilitating environment.

Guided by these premises, Blank and Solomon developed a specialized language program composed of short, individual tutoring sessions, with special emphasis on

1. selective attention
2. relevant inner verbalization
3. categories of exclusion
4. imagery of future events
5. separation of the world from its effect
6. models for cause and effect reasoning
7. ability to categorize
8. awareness of possessing language
9. sustained sequential thinking

When children from this specialized program were compared with children from a regular nursery school and with children from a tutorial program that had individual sessions but no specialized training, results showed a marked gain in IQ score for the group from the program designed by Blank and Solomon and no significant gains for the others.

What can we make of this work? We can view it in one of two general ways. First, the skills being taught highly reflect

behaviors peculiar to middle-class existence. This is not to
underestimate their importance for groups other than the
middle class. But, assuming the previously discussed connection between group membership and the skills most valued, it
is not surprising to find that intensive practice on these skills
leads to IQ gains. And this fact raises the covert difficulty
that items on IQ tests may be biased toward the skills prized
by the middle class.

The work of Blank and Solomon can also be viewed as
follows: The skills they seek to activate are prized no matter
what culture one belongs to. But apparently these skills do
not belong in great measure to the minority children studied
by Blank and Solomon. Is this a matter for embarrassment or
anger? Oppressed minorities, by virtue of their oppression,
have precious little motivation to exercise such skills as long
attention span, long-range future planning, or employment of
models for cause-and-effect abstraction. This of course may
be too strong a characterization since it implies that nowhere
in the mental life of minority groups can one find strong
evidence for highly elaborated plans and creative thinking.
Such a strong view would of course be wrong in the sense
that the content on which such skills are exercised may be
very different in the various subcultures. The formal testing
situation highlighted by Blank and Solomon may be teaching
these special skills for only a certain content. The minority
children studied may only appear to lack these skills because
the proper content valued by their subgroup has not been
tapped. We admit to sheer speculation in this regard but we
mention it in order to illustrate how an ethnographic
orientation can provide one with a touchstone to guide one's
analysis of cognitive functioning in various subcultures.

Gray and Klaus (1965) report on their Early Training
Project, which attempted to fight the "progressive retardation" of deprived children by manipulating several variables

that previous research had indicated were influential. These variables included broadening spatial and temporal organization and the restrictive language code of mother-child interaction; providing a high adult-to-child ratio, high verbal interaction, and individualized instruction; focusing on motivational-attitude variables, such as achievement motivation, identification with achieving roles, delay of gratification, and interest in school activities; and cognitive development factors, such as perception, concept formation, and language.

The subjects admitted to the program consisted of black children from a city in the Upper South, chosen to meet criteria related to housing, parental education, and occupation. Three groups were formed: T(1), which had three summers of a ten-week preschool program and three years of weekly home visits; T(2), which had two summers of the program and two years of the weekly home visits; and T(3), which was a control group. The authors added T(4) as another control in a distant, similar city. The children in each group were pre- and posttested on a variety of measures, including the SB, the WISC, the ITPA, and the PPVT. The treatment groups performed better than the control groups on all subtests, which indicated general improvement. On tests of various attitudinal measures, differences were in the expected direction but did not reach significance. The authors concluded that the improvements were sustained although the gains maintained over the four years were modest. All groups jumped and then declined in performance after the second year of school, but they maintained their relative positions. The authors were optimistic about overcoming progressive retardation, provided that massive changes in homes and schools could be accomplished.

This work is reminiscent of Blank and Solomon. A seeming elevation in performance was miraculously acquired by the children. But, the bubble burst as their performance declined. What are the ethnographic dynamics of this? The decline in performance is probably due to a mismatch in the temporary skills they brought to training and those they actually use in their everyday lives. This raises an enormous difficulty with the function of educational institutions in minority group settings. If our view is right, education cannot progress and take firm hold until the institutions responsible for it build upon the skills of those they wish to educate. Support for our interpretation here can be found in several recent works, for example, Cazden, John-Steiner, and Hymes (1972); McDermott (1974, 1975); and Rist (1973).

We infer that many of the authors of the studies cited believe that test scores bear a simple cause-effect relation to the test item. They do not. Another objection, in addition to those we have stated, is that subjects responding to test items bring to the task a cultural expectation of the type of answer they are expected to give—cultural knowledge they have learned primarily outside formal examination situations. In particular, subcultural groups bring to the task a healthy suspicion concerning the motives for their being tested. Models are needed to describe information-processing steps which show the flow of prior expectation and knowledge, semantic readings of the content of test items, memory-search processes of their knowledge stores, and processes leading to a response. Even though many of these authors cannot truly be held accountable for this kind of analysis, in our view it is still a critical concern for achieving an accurate characterization of an interpretation of why differences occur in test performance.

Rate of Change and Sentence Recall

In most every instance, the studies on intellectual performance and problem solving have employed traditional measures to validate their assumptions. Hall and Freedle (1973) subjected their sentence-recall data (reported earlier; see Figure 2 in particular) to a rate-of-change measure as a new means of deriving an aspect of cognitive ability. Most studies report measures of the number of correct answers or the number of errors as input to their analyses. Across age groups there is an additional manipulation to be made of such scores, namely, rate of improvement, which we feel carries important information for comparison across subcultural groups. The next section discusses how the rate measure can be calculated. An interpretation using the device follows.

An Equation for Determining the Significance of the Rate-of-Change Parameter a

Statistics texts give a standard result for determining the variance of a statistic when the sample size is very large, which is known as finding the formula for the asymptotic variance of a parameter a. The particular parameter we are interested in comes from the linear equation

$$P_2 = P_1 + a(1 - P_1) \qquad (1)$$

which says that the quantity P_2 (the proportion of correct repetitions at age 10) is assumed to result from the quantity correct at an earlier time period P_1 (that is, P_1 would be the number of corrects at age 8, say) plus a proportion a of the quantity $1 - P$. The parameter A can be regarded as a rate of change over two time periods. Given that we have data which allow us to get sample estimates of the quantities P_1 and P_2, from which we estimate the quantity a, we seek to compare this resulting magnitude with another similarly calculated quantity resulting from another independent estimate of P_1 and P_2 obtained from another population of subjects.

The result of obtaining variance statistics for the quantity a will allow us to test the following idea: Is the rate of change for white subjects in responding correctly to SE sentences any different from the rate of change for black subjects responding to the same sentences? A similar question can then be raised about the rates of change in responding to BEV sentences. Similar questions can be addressed to the problem of whether 8-to-10-year-old lower-class blacks are faster (or slower) in their rate-of-change parameter in responding to BEV forms in comparison with middle-class blacks. The question for whites would be whether those from the lower class are any different from their middle-class counterparts in rates of change when responding to SE forms.

The asymptotic variance of a is given by the following equation

$$a = \left(\frac{P_2 - P}{1 - P_1}\right) \rightarrow \eta \left[\frac{P_2 - P_1}{1 - P_1}, \left(\frac{P_2(1 - P_2)}{n_2} + \frac{P_1(1 - P_1)}{n_1}\right)\left(\frac{1}{(1 - P_1)^2}\right)\right]$$

(2)

where η represents the normal distribution with mean equal to $(P_2 - P_1)/(1 - P_1)$ with variance V_1 equal to

$$\left(\frac{P_2(1 - P_2)}{n_2} + \frac{P_1(1 - P_1)}{n_1}\right)\left(\frac{1}{(1 - P_1)^2}\right) \quad (3)$$

Note that n_2 represents the number of observations that went into the calculation of the quantity P_2 while n_1 represents the number of observations used in calculating the quantity P_1.

A similar quantity is calculated from another pair of observations of P_2 and P_1 to estimate another rate-of-change parameter a. In order to distinguish these values from the other values, let us place a prime on them as follows.

$$a' = \left(\frac{P_2' - P_1'}{1 - P_1'}\right) \rightarrow \eta\left[\frac{P_2' - P_1'}{1 - P_1'}, \left(\frac{P_2'(1 - P_2')}{n_2'}\right.\right.$$

$$\left.\left. + \frac{P_1'(1 - P_1')}{n_1'}\right)\left(\frac{1}{(1 - P_1')^2}\right)\right] \tag{4}$$

Let us designate the variance part of this equation for a' by the symbol V_2. Now we wish to test whether these two independent estimates of a and a' are significantly different from each other. The equation to test this is

$$\left(\frac{a - a'}{\sqrt{V_1 + V_2}}\right) \rightarrow \eta(0, 1) \tag{5}$$

which means that the test is made with respect to the normal distribution with mean 0.0 and variance 1.0.

Comparison of Rates of Change for Data on Correct Responses

Using these statistics we find that blacks are not significantly different from whites in their rate of improvement in responding to standard English sentences ($z = 0.147$). If we interpret this rate-of-improvement parameter as reflecting underlying abilities in memory, comprehension of language, etc., then we may feel that we are justified in drawing the conclusion that blacks are not inferior to whites in their learning ability. They do differ from whites, of course, in that at age 8 they do not get as many standard sentences correct as do whites. But the rate-of-change parameter is not dependent upon the starting proportions P_1. It is a measure of rate of *change* in improvement over two time periods and as such is independent of the starting proportions. The learning parameter a for whites was .489 while that for blacks was .497.

We can calculate another pair of parameters for the rate at which blacks improve in responding to BEV sentences over ages 8 to 10 and compare this with the rate of change with respect to whites' improvement in responding to BEV sentences. The result of this calculation indicates that at ages 8 to 10 blacks respond correctly to BEV sentences at a significantly higher rate than whites ($z = 3.405$). The a was .171 for blacks and .052 for whites. The meaning of this result is less clear than that of the first calculation since whites do not get much exposure to black dialect or feel any cultural pressure to learn it; hence, the higher learning rate of blacks in response to BEV may primarily reflect opportunities to learn it. But this cannot be the full story! We see that blacks have a greater opportunity to gain greater competence in black dialect from the ages of 8 to 10, yet their learning rate for BEV is only .171 in comparison with a significantly higher rate of .497 for SE. This suggests that the learning rates among blacks reflect a complex number of factors including responsiveness to the cultural pressure to speak SE and, by implication, a corresponding pressure to stop speaking BEV. The smaller learning rate of .171 for nonstandard sentences may reflect a complex mixture of abilities, such as greater memory capacity at the later age and greater familiarity with and comprehension of these structures, which on the one hand tend to increase this rate; but, in addition, the rate reflects an even more powerful pressure for social conformity which works to *depress* the rate measure. Hence the rate measure ends up significantly smaller for BEV than it does for SE.

Another interesting comparison that bears comment is the contrast within the blacks according to socioeconomic level. For SE the lower-class blacks yielded a rate of improvement of .431 and middle-class a rate of .578. This difference, which is significant, may reflect a complex of factors. The middle-class blacks appear to be more highly motivated or more willing than the lower-class blacks to gain competence in the standard forms. The lower-class blacks may show a combination of greater antagonism to the standard forms with somewhat less direct contact with standard speakers; the consequence of this is lower motivation and less opportunity for gaining great competence in standard English. This argument seems to hold up when we examine the learning rates for the lower- and middle-class whites in response to standard English. The lower class had an a of .481 as compared with the middle class, whose a was .505; this difference is not significant. Our reason for outlining this pattern again has to do with concepts of cultural pressure. Since both white groups have always spoken predominantly SE and since there is no corresponding pressure to learn the BEV forms (even among lower-class whites), there is no reason to expect that the two white groups will differ in their learning rates. Our argument falls somewhat short of the mark, however, when we contrast the learning rates of the two white groups on BEV. Here the lower-class whites, who should do better than the middle-class whites, yield an a equal only to .052, while the middle-class whites yield an a of .107. This difference is significant and thus presents us with a puzzle, which at the moment we are unable to explain. However, a similar contrast for BEV between lower-class blacks ($a = .220$) and middle-class blacks ($a = .110$) is significantly different. This presumably can be explained by postulating that lower-class blacks have had greater opportunity to gain competence in BEV usage than have those from the middle class.

A final comment about the rate-of-change parameter a may be of value here. Some readers may question in what sense one can claim that the estimate of a need not be correlated with the starting proportion P_1. The form of Eq.

(1) allows us to assert that if improvement at a later time (P_2) is never worse than at the earlier time (P_1), then the parameter a will be free to take on values between and including 0.0 and 1.0. This range of values of a is in no way influenced by the starting value of P_1 except in the very exceptional case where P_1 happens to represent perfect performance (i.e., where $P_1 = 1.0$). It is in the sense described here that we assert that the improvement parameter a is independent of the starting value.

Moreover, it may appear to some that even though two values of a (estimated from different groups, such as blacks and whites) are equal, one should not conclude that the amount of work that has to be done by the two groups of subjects to get these same a values is necessarily equivalent. This is certainly true. Let us pursue this point further, since it will even strengthen our claim that blacks can at least equal whites in this measure (and perhaps outstrip them, as we shall now demonstrate). Suppose that whites do very well on standard English at age 8, that for example their $P_1 = .80$ (they get 80 percent of the standard structures correct at age 8). Now suppose that the improvement parameter a for these same subjects is .5. Applying Eq. (1), we see that at age 10 they will get 90 percent of the standard structures correct since $.80 + .5(1 - .80) = .90$.

Now let us contrast this example with blacks who start at a lower level of correct performance on standard forms (have a lower P_1 value of, say, .40) but who show the same value on their improvement parameter a of .5 over ages 8 to 10. We see by applying Eq. (1) that their percentage of correct performance at age 10 will be .70, since $.4 + .5(1 - .4) = .70$. Notice that in an absolute sense these blacks have had to cover more ground in order to earn this improvement parameter of .5 than did the whites. That is, the blacks have had to improve by 30 percent while the whites have had to improve by only 10 percent in order to earn the same learning parameter. From this point of view, even though the blacks still lag behind the whites in their absolute level of correct performance on standard forms at age 10 (i.e., the blacks still get only 70 percent correct at age 10, while the whites get 90 percent), the total amount of learning that the blacks have had to engage in to earn this rate-of-change parameter of .5 was nevertheless much greater than the absolute amount of learning that the whites have had to engage in to earn the same .5 parameter. Thus, in spite of the fact that blacks lag behind whites in absolute performance at each age, in another sense they are superior to whites inasmuch as they were capable of learning a much larger piece of the "linguistic pie" in order to earn the identical parameter of .5. Clearly, the manner in which one chooses to score the protocols in experimental settings (and by implication, the manner in which one wishes to score blacks on some standardized tests) can greatly affect the interpretation of the data! We suggest that greater attention be paid to rates of improvement as useful scores for assessing the functioning of various racial and socioeconomic groups, especially since these rate-of-change parameters seem to tell quite a different story from conventional measures, which typically examine only the absolute level of performance such as total percent correct at some specific age.

SUMMARY

Jensen's hypothesis that blacks are genetically inferior was discussed. A critique was provided which indicates that Jensen's interpretation is quite insensitive to the power that culture has in molding and directing its members to utilize and develop their mental resources. Additional studies which are tangentially related to the Jensen controversy were also

SELF-CONCEPT

Since this book is primarily about black language, one might ask why we address ourselves to the black self-concept. Earlier we stated our belief that one must interpret language usage from a large conceptual framework so as to implicate the social sphere in communication. It seems axiomatic to us that the social milieu helps one to define his self-concept, and the self-concept that evolves affects the manner in which one person communicates with another. For example, if a black person's self-concept is negative, such an attitude is revealed when that person interacts with other blacks in their subculture; and it will show up in other variants when the black interacts with members of the mainstream culture. In line with our earlier contrast of wholistic cultures versus

This part is based on a previous work "Stages in the Development of a Black Identity," by William S. Hall, Roy Freedle, and William E. Cross, Jr. It appeared as *ACT Research Report* No. 50, April 1972, and was copyrighted by The American College Testing Program, Iowa City, Iowa. Permission to reproduce Tables 3, 4, 5, 6, and 7 [Tables 14–18 in the present book] from this report has graciously been given by The American College Testing Program.

embedded subcultures, we propose that the notion of self-concept can help to clarify the variety of speech patterns that members of the subculture may employ. In this section we will first enlist certain facts to characterize how blacks perceive themselves and then we will attempt to deduce the possible consequences this may have for language use.

It is unfortunate that studies are not available that simultaneously examine language communication patterns and an individual's self-concept. Perhaps this is not surprising since psycholinguists have only recently begun to realize that language does not function in a vacuum, but is intimately tied to the total knowledge system of an individual. (A knowledge system includes emotional attitudes toward other members of one's subgroup, toward oneself, and toward others outside one's subgroup.) Given this limitation of the literature, we can only hint at the interesting possible connections between self-concept and language.

Most of the early work in this area treats the black self-concept in terms of what Hall, Freedle, and Cross (1972) have characterized as stage 1—the person sees himself in terms of negative attitudes. It will be useful first to discuss the Hall, Freedle, and Cross work because it provides us with a viewpoint that is both historical and contemporary, which will in turn help us place in context numerous studies of the black self-concept, beginning with the work done in the 1940s.

The 1954 Supreme Court decision that outlawed segregation in the nation's schools has contributed to a change in the nature of the embedded subcultural experience. If a fully articulated theory of how the subcultural experience ties in with cognition were available, it would be theoretically possible to predict and document cognitive changes in members of the affected subcultures. In lieu of such a theory, Hall, Freedle, and Cross (1972) hypothesized a link between a systematic growth in attitude organization and changes in the subcultural experience. They therefore sought to document a relationship between cognitive organization and cultural press. We shall present this work in some detail.

FOUR STAGES OF BLACK IDENTITY TRANSFORMATION

Through careful analysis of his observations of a wide segment of the black American community, Cross (1970) hypothesized that there exists a series of well-defined stages through which black Americans pass when they encounter blackness in themselves. Moreover, he speculated that as a result of this encounter and its subsequent resolution, the person defines himself as a black, adequate, and noninferior person. He designated the stages as follows:

Pre-encounter (stage 1): In this stage, some experience manages to slip by or even shatter the person's current feelings about himself and his interpretation of the condition of the Negro.

Encounter (stage 2): During this period, a person discovers what it is like to be black.

Immersion (stage 3): During this period, everything of value must be relevant to blackness.

Internalization (stage 4): In this stage, the individual focuses on things other than himself and his own ethnic or racial group.

That a transformation in the black American's awareness has occurred will be readily acknowledged by most people; but that fact does not in itself verify the notion that the experience occurs in discrete stages, nor does it verify the particular values and ideas asserted by Cross and others to be characteristic of each stage. To merely list some values and ideas believed to underlie or characterize each stage brings us closer to the goal of empirically establishing the psychological reality of this phenomenon; but it certainly does not finish the job.

THE HALL-FREEDLE-CROSS STUDY

Consensual Validation

Hall, Freedle, and Cross (1972) approached an empirical test of Cross's hypothesis by what they called *consensual validation*. Let us summarize their reasoning.

They accepted the notion that black college students have had intimate knowledge and experience with the four stages, i.e., that they have known or know many blacks who have been through several of the various stages and that the blacks who serve as subjects will have stored up numerous facts and impressions about the behavior of such individuals. It is thus not essential to assume that college blacks are themselves in the fourth stage in order for them to perform adequately in the Hall-Freedle-Cross experiment.

Now let us suppose that these subjects are presented with statements that Cross believes to be characteristic of the stage of black identity transformation. If these statements are accurate reflections of beliefs about the black identity process, then it should be possible to show high agreement (consensual validation) among the black subjects regarding which items belong together in characterizing each stage. Furthermore, it may be possible to determine, through experimental conditions, how many of these stages exist.

The 28 items suggested by Cross as representing the different beliefs and activities of the four stages were presented to subjects for sorting (see Table 14). The effects

TABLE 14

Summary of item responses

	Blacks				Whites				Item description
	A	B	C	D	A	B	C	D	
1.	883	067	017	033	900	033	033	033	"... the world is, and should be, guided by American-European concepts..."
2.	967	017	000	017	967	017	000	017	"... to be black is to be lowdown and dirty."
3.	950	017	000	033	817	117	050	017	"... black people came from a strange, uncivilized dark continent...."
4.	933	033	017	017	983	000	000	017	"... white esthetic is superior to the black one...."
5.	950	017	000	033	902	016	016	066	"... white man is superior intellectually, technically mystical, and capable of understanding him."
6.	949	017	017	017	917	033	000	050	"... large numbers of blacks are untrustworthy."
7.	593	271	068	068	467	017	100	317	"... incorporation, integration, or assimilation is the black man's most effective weapon for solving his problems."
8.	033	098	721	148	033	283	583	100	"... interprets the world from a black perspective."
9.	017	339	322	322	000	407	390	203	"...validate[s] himself as a black person...."
10.	233	450	233	083	117	567	300	017	"... feel[s] guilty and anxious; consequently, he is hurled into a frantic, determined, obsessive search for black identity."

See note at end of table, page 135.

133

TABLE 14

Summary of item responses (*continued*)

| | Proportion of 60 students who placed this item in stages A, B, C, or D | | | | | | | |
	Blacks				Whites				Item description
	A	B	C	D	A	B	C	D	
11.	000	390	169	441	017	333	267	383	"... feels with great force what being black in America means."
12.	017	100	717	167	000	233	650	117	"... involves himself in a world of blackness: e.g., he participates in political meetings, rapping sessions. . . ."
13.	017	186	644	153	033	283	633	050	"... undergoes a liberation from whiteness. . . ."
14.	067	200	500	233	067	283	533	117	"... feels and behaves as if the white world, culture, and persons are dehuman. . . ."
15.	000	183	700	117	000	283	583	133	"... feels that everything black is good."
16.	033	200	650	117	000	317	650	033	"... consumes black literature and devotes much contemplation to the forms of being black. . . ."
17.	083	200	533	183	067	317	500	117	"... turns inward and withdraws from everything that is white."
18.	068	237	339	356	067	200	267	467	"... frequently confronts the system and the man."
19.	033	167	250	550	033	133	300	533	"... indicate[s] that he fears neither control nor oppressive techniques nor death."
20.	000	133	417	450	017	333	550	100	"... feels an overwhelming attachment to all black people."

Item								
21	017	133	**500**	350	017	350	**450**	183
22	083	317	017	**483**	033	250	267	**450**
23	000	283	**500**	217	000	**525**	288	186
24	083	**367**	200	350	016	197	246	**541**
25	067	217	217	**500**	000	117	200	**683**
26	050	083	167	**700**	082	033	082	**803**
27	033	167	217	**583**	000	100	100	**767**
28	000	050	367	**583**	000	033	233	**733**

21. "... feels excitement and joy in black surroundings."
22. "... begins to see whites as just people with the strengths and limitations that this perception implies."
23. "... engages in a cultural analysis of black life style."
24. "... comes to accept certain factors about the black experience and drops others."
25. "... has accepted certain factors that help explain the experience of being black in America and incorporated these into a style of life which forms the basis for a new life style."
26. "... behaves as if he has an inner security and satisfaction with himself."
27. "... feels a great love and compassion for all oppressed people."
28. "... actively participates in the community for the purpose of making it better, i.e., a collectivistic orientation with a commitment to the development of black power dominates the person's behavior."

Note. Items 1 through 7 correspond to Cross's first stage; items 8 through 11 correspond to his second stage; items 12 through 25 to his third stage; and items 26 through 28 to his fourth stage. The boldface numbers represent the modal responses for each item for blacks and whites considered separately. One can see an impressive similarity between stages considered as the modal response for virtually all items except items 20, 23, and 24. Notice too that we can revise Cross's hypothesis regarding which particular items belong in each of the four stages by using the modal judgments of the 60 black students. For example, under the revised hypothesis we should place items 1 through 7 in the first stage (this exactly coincides with Cross's first stage). Items 9, 10, and 24 would go in the second stage; items 8, 12, 13, 14, 15, 16, 17, 21, and 23 would go in the third stage; and items 11, 18, 19, 20, 22, 25, 26, 27, and 28 would go in the fourth stage.

of three experimental conditions (A, B, and C) on the sorting of these items were studied.

Condition A represented the fewest constraints on subjects who sorted the items. The subjects were instructed as follows: "On these cards you will find some items descriptive of a person—taken together, many of these items form clusters. We want you to cluster the items according to whether a person would believe all of the items that are in the cluster at a particular point in his life—whereas the items in another cluster would tend to be believed by him at some other point in his life. After sorting the items into clusters, indicate the order in which you feel these clusters occur in time." They were further asked to think of a name for each of the clusters.

Condition B placed somewhat greater constraints on the subjects than did condition A. Following the first sort, the subjects were asked if there was any meaningful way in which they could recombine or regroup any of their original clusters so that only four clusters remained. If the subject had already produced four clusters on his first sort, the session was terminated. Following each sort, the subjects were again asked to order the clusters with respect to their temporal sequence and were also asked to give a reason for each group of items they produced.

Condition C placed the greatest constraint upon the subjects. Four boxes were placed in front of each subject. Each box had placed next to it a label which described the nature of the four stages and the order in which they were believed to occur as expressed by Cross's hypothesis. The descriptions which followed each label were aimed at clarifying the meaning of each stage and thereby served to remove much of the uncertainty as to what the sorting task was all about.

A total of 180 subjects were tested. There were an equal number of black and white college students. Within each group of 90, 30 were tested in condition A, 30 in condition B, and 30 in condition C. Finally, each group of 30 was equally divided by sex, 15 females and 15 males. Each subject was tested individually. The test session for each condition lasted about an hour.

Results and Discussion

Conditions B (Four-Cluster Sortings) and C

Conditions B and C will be analyzed because they provided the most detailed information regarding the distribution of the items with respect to each of the four hypothetical stages. For purposes of illustrating the method of analysis clearly, let us suppose that Cross had used only six items (A, B, C, D, E, and F) instead of 28 and had grouped them into only two temporal stages such that items A and B belonged to the first stage and items C, D, E, and F belonged to the second stage. Suppose, furthermore, that a student who was asked to sort these six items into two clusters placed items A, B, and C into the first cluster and items D, E, and F into the second; and that he ordered the two clusters with respect to their occurrence in time. Because the subject had ordered the cluster to correspond to a time scale, one could assign a median rank to each item placed in the first cluster and another median rank to each item placed in the second cluster. For example, items A, B, and C would each get a median rank of 2 and items D, E, and F would each get a median rank of 5. The experimenter could assign median ranks as well to the six items grouped according to the much-simplified Cross hypothesis. Because only items A and B were placed in the first stage, each item would receive a median rank of 1.5 and the remaining four items would receive a median rank of 4.5. The rank-order correlation between this subject's clustering responses and the simplified Cross hypothesis could be readily computed.

Now let us carry the argument one step further. If instead of merely one student's responses, 30 students' responses to each of these six items were considered, the group data could be summarized in the following way. For item A, one could indicate how many subjects placed it into the first stage and how many placed it into the second stage by the notation (20, 10); this notation means that 20 subjects placed the item in the first cluster and 10 placed it in the second cluster. The modal response for item A would be the first cluster (stage) because the greatest number of subjects placed it there. Similarly for item B, suppose that we have (18, 12); then the modal response for this item is also the first stage. The point of this argument is that by using the group data one could also calculate the rank-order correlation of these data with the simplified Cross hypothesis. This process greatly simplifies the presentation of the data. With the full 28 items and four stages within which to distribute the subjects' responses, there were very few ties (only three ties out of 224 decisions in assigning a modal response). For these ties, the modal stage was chosen randomly.

The rank-order correlations with the 28-item Cross hypothesis for each of eight groups of subjects (male and female white subjects in condition B, male and female black subjects in condition B, male and female white subjects in condition C, and male and female black subjects in condition C) can be found in Table 15. All correlations between each of the eight groups and the Cross hypothesis were significant well beyond the .01 level. Only one of the eight groups (condition B, white females, group O), seemed to produce a slightly lower correlation with the Cross hypothesis. What is

TABLE 15

Rank-order correlation of each of eight groups with the
Cross hypothesis and with each other

	Condition B				Condition C				Cross hypothesis
	Whites		Blacks		Whites		Blacks		
	M	F	M	F	M	F	M	F	V
	N	O	P	Q	R	S	T	U	V
N	1.000	.715	.743	.922	.918	.929	.763	.876	.840
O	.715	1.000	.596	.668	.699	.661	.491	.756	.560
P	.743	.596	1.000	.799	.831	.714	.790	.737	.750
Q	.922	.668	.799	1.000	.920	.893	.705	.831	.810
R	.918	.699	.831	.920	1.000	.897	.798	.830	.820
S	.929	.661	.714	.893	.897	1.000	.776	.807	.850
T	.763	.491	.790	.705	.798	.776	1.000	.697	.860
U	.876	.756	.737	.831	.830	.807	.697	1.000	.730
V	.840	.560	.750	.810	.820	.850	.860	.730	1.000

Note. A correlation of .448 is needed to be significant at the .01 level (one-tailed test).

also of note in Table 15 is that the intercorrelations between each pair of the groups of subjects were generally very high. What might have been expected is that the intercorrelations between the four groups run within the same condition would be higher than correlations across groups from different conditions. Little evidence was found for this viewpoint. It appears that despite the fact that subjects in condition C were provided labels for each of the four stages as well as information about the temporal order in which these were believed to occur, their correlations with the Cross hypothesis were at about the same magnitude as subjects in condition B.

The tentative conclusion reached at this point was that using only the modal response data, we found significant evidence that supported the general ideas of Cross. However, the fact that none of the correlations was perfect indicated that some differences must be occurring within each group of subjects. The differences relate to how many as well as what particular items were placed within each of the allowable four stages.

In order to gain further insight into the source of the differences, a more detailed comparison across items was made. The analysis focused on possible differences in black-white response patterns for each item within and across conditions B and C. In the interest of providing a more stable response pattern base, the male and female frequency data of conditions B and C were combined. These pooled data were used for the remainder of the analyses.

Condition B: Black-White Comparisons (Four-Cluster Data Only)

Of the 28-item comparisons which tested differences in patterns of clustering between black and white subjects, only item 7 produced a significant difference by application of the

Kolmogorov-Smirnov two-sample test ($p < .01$). This item asserts that "incorporation, integration, or assimilation is the black man's most effective weapon for solving his problems." The 30 black subjects perceived this as belonging primarily to the first developmental stage (pre-encounter) while the 30 whites were equally split between those who perceived it as representing an early stage and those who perceived it as representing a late stage; none of the remaining 27 items produced a difference ($p > .05$). This significant difference for item 7 cannot necessarily be inferred from the data summarized in Table 14, because the table pools the data across conditions B and C.

Condition C: Black-White Comparisons

This condition produced more significant differences in the item responses of blacks and whites. The Kolmogorov-Smirnov two-sample test was used again on each of the 28 items.

Item 20 was different at the .01 level. Whites placed this item primarily in the third stage (immersion) and most blacks placed it in the fourth stage (internalization).

Item 24 was significantly different at the .05 level. The whites' modal response was to place this item in the fourth stage; blacks revealed a bimodal response pattern by placing it equally often in the second and the fourth stages. (It is possible that this item may have an ambiguous reading since it does not assert which specific factors are to be accepted and which are to be dropped.)

Finally, item 28 produced a significant difference at the .05 level. This difference, however, is less interesting than the differences previously found because both blacks and whites gave the fourth stage as their modal response category. The difference was presumably due to the unequal variances of the two frequency distributions (the Kolmogorov-Smirnov test is sensitive not only to differences in central tendency of the responsive frequency distributions but also to relative variance, skewness, etc.).

Comparisons across Conditions B and C

We have concentrated so far on item differences attributable to variations in groups of students. One can also ask whether significant item differences can be found when comparing across conditions B and C. Differences might be expected for the following reasons: When a semantic label for each of the four stages is provided (as was the case for condition C), this should greatly decrease whatever ambiguity there is to the sorting task. The consequence of reducing the ambiguity or uncertainty is that more students should agree to place a particular item into only one of the stages. That is to say, if a particular item belongs to (or is characteristic of) a particular stage, then providing information about the meaning of the stage should help to increase the number of students who will match that item with that particular stage.

The possibility was investigated from two points of view. The first examined whether a difference in the frequency distributions of each item were significant across conditions B and C. The second tested directly the implication that the modal frequency of each item in condition C was significantly larger than its corresponding modal frequency in condition B by using four-cluster data only.

The frequency distributions of the 30 black students in condition B were compared with the frequency distributions of the 30 black students from condition C, item for item. Of the 28 Kolmogorov-Smirnov two-sample tests only two were significant, item 14 ($p < .05$) and item 27 ($p < .05$). Of these two, only item 14 involved a change in modal response category. Condition B produced a modal response for the fourth stage, and condition C produced a modal response for the third stage.

Using the same test, the frequency distributions of the 30 white subjects in condition B were compared with the frequency distributions of the 30 white subjects in condition C. Five of the 28-item comparisons were found to be significantly different from chance; these were items 13, 15, 16, 27, and 28. Only one of these (item 15) involved a change in the modal response, where the second stage was modal for condition B and the third stage was modal for condition C.

Although there were more items which yielded significant differences than could be attributed to chance, the failure of these differences to form any systematic pattern across conditions and across black-white comparisons suggested that most of these differences may not be very important in terms of what impact they have on the main hypothesis concerning the existence of several stages underlying the development of black awareness. The few differences found between the black and white students, however, may be important for reasons other than the stages hypothesis.

A second approach in evaluating differences between conditions B and C was also considered. The modal frequencies in condition C were predicted to be greater than the corresponding modal frequencies in condition B. (Only the items that share the same modal category were considered for this test.) A sign test of the difference, using the black subjects' responses across the two conditions, was significant ($p = .022$). A similar sign test using only the white subjects' responses across the same conditions was also significantly different from chance ($p = .001$). The result thus indicated that the ability to place an item into its correct stage was significantly increased by having available a semantic label for each stage.

Existence of a Generalization Gradient
among the Four Stages

If we suppose that the four stages can be ordered along a one-dimensional scale, then it is possible to argue that different amounts of confusion should exist, especially between adjacent stages on this one dimension. The degree of this confusion will depend in part on how close together these stages are located on the dimension; if they are very close together they will tend to be confused more often than if they are far apart. We will consider this notion in more detail.

Let us assume that a particular item is known to belong to the third stage and that a large number of subjects pick up this item and are about to place it into one of the four clusters. Most of the subjects should place the item correctly, but when one errs, he or she will likely misplace it in a stage closest (in the temporal scale sense) to the correct stage. That is, if the third stage is known to be correct, then most of the items will be placed in the third stage (the modal stage); the next most frequent entry will be in either the second or the fourth stage (because they are nearest to the third stage on the time scale). The least frequent entry would be placing the item in the first stage.

To give another example, if the correct stage is known to be the fourth one, then the greatest proportion of subjects will place the item in the fourth stage; the next largest proportion will place it in the third stage; the next largest, the second; and the smallest, the first.

In order to evaluate this idea against the present set of data, we must be able to estimate the degrees to which this generalization gradient around the correct stage can occur by chance alone. This is easy to determine. We use the integers 1, 2, 3, and 4 to represent four different magnitudes. There are 24 different ways to permute these four different magnitudes: **1234**, **1243**, 1324, **1342**, 1423, **1432**, 2134, 2143, 2314, **2341**, 2413, **2431**, 3124, 3142, 3214, 3241, 3412, **3421**, 4123, 4132, 4213, 4231, 4312, and **4321**. Exactly eight of these 24 permutations satisfy the concept of a generalization gradient idea. The largest number in this is 4, which occurs in the third position (analagous to saying that the modal response is for the third stage). The next largest number, 3, is adjacent to 4; the third largest number, 2, is also adjacent to 4; and the smallest number, 1, is farthest from 4. Hence, all these magnitudes decrease quite regularly around the largest (modal) number. The same is true for all the boldface numbers in the sequence. Since exactly 8 out of 24 possible orderings satisfy the gradient on the basis of chance alone, the expected proportion due to chance is equal to .333. Table 16 shows that the data yield proportions well above this base line. By a sign test using the eight groups of subjects, the result is significant at the $p = .004$ level. Hence, the data clearly give evidence for the presence of a generalization gradient around the correct modal responses. (In this test, only the items that gave four distinct numbers were included in determining the observed proportion; i.e., tied entries were not allowed because they greatly complicate the carrying out of the test.) By a further inference, the existence of the generalization gradient implies that the four stages lie on a temporal scale. The earliest stage lies at the left extreme of the scale (the pre-encounter stage); the next stage to the right is the encounter stage; the next stage to the right is the immersion stage; and finally, at the right end of the scale is the internalization stage.

One conclusion that can be drawn from the existence of the generalization gradient is that the subjects in the experiment have properly ordered the items representing the four stages according to Cross's original hypothesis. Had they

TABLE 16

Evidence for the existence of a generalization
gradient for each of eight groups of subjects

Group of subjects	Obtained proportion of items showing the generalization gradient	Expected proportion of items showing the gradient due to chance
Condition B		
Black males	.769	.333
Black females	.684	.333
White males	.933	.333
White females	.789	.333
Condition C		
Black males	.812	.333
Black females	.625	.333
White males	.750	.333
White females	.692	.333

Note. A sign test (one-tailed) which compares the direction of
the obtained proportion with the proportion expected by chance
alone indicates that the evidence given here in favor of the existence of
the generalization gradient is significant at the .004 level.

not ordered the stages in the correct temporal order, the
generalization test would have failed to be significant.

Suggested Item Revisions

A Revised Item List for the Four Cross Stages

We have already pointed out that general support for the
plausibility of Cross's hypothesis can be inferred from the
large significant rank-order correlations reported earlier in
this discussion. However, the more detailed item analyses and
the modal response patterns (especially those of the 60 black
subjects given in Table 14) indicate that some revision or

restatement of Cross's hypothesis should be considered. First of all, the present modal data suggests that the following items should be in each of the four stages:

Stage 1 should include items 1 through 7 (which coincides exactly with Cross's original suggested grouping).
Stage 2 should include items 9, 10, and 24.
Stage 3 should include items 8, 12, 13, 14, 15, 16, 17, 21, and 23.
Stage 4 should include items 11, 18, 19, 20, 22, 25, 26, 27, and 28.

Although the white subjects' modal responses suggest a rather similar reordering, it is open to question whether their perception of the items (and their lack of first-hand experience with these stages) was as accurate as that of the black subjects. Hence, we do not list here the ordering of Cross's hypothesis using the white subjects' data; the interested reader is referred to the summary data in Table 14.

Suggested Revisions in the Statement of Item Content

At various points in this section we have suggested there may be difficulty in interpreting the intent of some of the items. This difficulty was made apparent when significant differences for particular items were found between blacks' and whites' response patterns. We wish to consider the nature of some possible revisions here.

In particular, item 9 is unusual in the sense that the black subjects tended to place it about equally often in each of the last three stages. A similar tendency was noted for the white subjects (see Table 14). This result suggests that the item is *not* clearly indicative of any single stage but is rather an activity that would be equally true of all three of the last stages. Hence, future studies of the present kind should consider eliminating this item. That is, when research focuses on items that are diagnostic of particular stages (and uses item responses to infer the existence of the stage concept), it is desirable to choose items that are most often placed into only one stage.

Item 11 also appears to yield an unusual frequency pattern: the modal response of both blacks and whites was the fourth stage, but the second most frequent response was the second stage. Apparently this item was ambiguous primarily because it did not focus attention on any single attribute of what being black in the United States means. Hence, in future tests the item either should be clarified with a list of particular attributes or should be deleted.

Another criticism of the item content is that some items tend to be stated in what has been called a double-barreled form. For example, item 19 asserts three different attributes as if they must necessarily go together. It seems quite possible, however, that some individuals who placed the item in the fourth stage (the modal response) might agree with the assertion that they do not fear "control" or "oppressive techniques," but the same individuals might definitely say that they fear death (death presumably at the hands of the oppressors, as it is implied by the full statement of the item). The authors did not fully appreciate the possibility of ambiguous reading of such items at the time the study was conducted. Future work should attempt to separate equivocal attributes and construct several items in place of the single item.

In retrospect, we do not think it inappropriate that the present study focused on a virtually verbatim statement of Cross's items as representative beliefs for the four stages. That is, an initial evaluation of such hypotheses should remain as faithful as possible to the original statements in order to properly say that one has given them a fair test. Now that we have shown that there is in all likelihood some general agreement regarding the existence of the stages and of some of the particular beliefs which characterize them, it is appropriate for future work to consider modifying the form and content of some of the items.

Results of Condition A and the
Initial Sortings of Condition B

The reason for allowing subjects in condition A to form as many clusters as they wished on their first sortings of the 28 items was an attempt to get some idea whether primarily four stages (clusters) would be spontaneously formed. The condition (and the initial sortings of the subjects in condition B, which placed no constraints on the number of clusters) forms the only evidence the authors have regarding the likelihood that the 28 items do or do not group themselves into primarily four clusters (stages). First, we tested to see whether the white subjects differed from the black subjects in the number of clusters they formed out of the 28 items (the test ignored the particular items placed in each cluster and counted only the number of different clusters formed). A Kolmogorov-Smirnov two-sample test (two-tailed) showed no significant difference between black and white subjects for either condition A ($p = .05$) or condition B ($p = .05$). The frequencies with which the different numbers of clusters were formed in the two conditions are given in Table 17. We see from this table that in condition A, 17 of the 60 subjects gave precisely four clusters in their initial sortings and 17 additional subjects gave five clusters. In condition B (first sortings only), the maximum was clearly five clusters, and the second most frequent entry was four clusters. This suggests two tentative conclusions. First, the hypothesis that four

TABLE 17

Frequency with which students yielded different number of clusters
on their first sortings for conditions A and B

Experimental condition	Number of clusters into which the 28 items were sorted																	Raw sum
	1	2	3	4	5	6	7	8	9	10	11	12	13	14	15	16	17	
A (blacks and whites pooled)	—	—	11	17	17	4	7	2	—	—	—	—	—	—	—	1	1	60
B (blacks and whites pooled)	—	—	10	15	20	5	4	2	—	1	1	—	—	2	—	—	—	60

Note. The black and white students' data were pooled because Kolmogorov-Smirnov two-sample tests indicated no significant difference either in condition A ($p > .05$, two-tailed) or in condition B ($p > .05$, two-tailed).

stages underlie the recent evolution of black awareness is approximately correct if we look at condition A results; and our hypothesis will be more open to questions if we concentrate on condition B results. Another possible conclusion is that there may be several alternate routes or belief systems by which one can gain conviction in the search for black identity. The answer to the latter possibility will have to await a method for analyzing the semantic labels or the reasons the subjects gave with respect to why they clustered items together.

Other Data

Table 18 presents a summary of the frequency with which each of the four stages was chosen for each item by 60 subjects in condition B (four-cluster data only) and condition C. The table pools the results of black and white students.

Toward the Construction of Quantitative Models

There is a general difficulty in developmental psychology in attempting to validate the notion of stage. We do not pretend to have solved this difficulty in the present study. But rather than dismiss the difficult problem in a summary fashion, let us consider some of its aspects that bear on the present issues.

Suppose we define a stage x such that the cognitive belief system of a person in that stage is fully characterized by a list of critical beliefs and attitudes. Let us designate these particular beliefs and attitudes by the symbols e, f, and g. Notice that the definition does not imply that the person cannot hold other beliefs as well. If we wish to exclude the possibility that a person in stage x does not believe statements h, i, and j, then we must modify the definition to read: A person is said to be in stage x if he fully endorses or

TABLE 18

Summary of item responses for conditions B and C

Item number	Frequency with which 60 students placed this item in stages A, B, C, or D							
	Condition B				Condition C			
	A	B	C	D	A	B	C	D
1	55	2	1	2	52	4	2	2
2	58	0	0	2	58	2	0	0
3	53	3	1	3	53	5	2	0
4	57	1	0	2	58	1	1	0
5	56	1	0	3	56	1	1	2
6	56	1	0	3	55	2	1	1
7	28	15	5	12	35	8	5	11
8	1	14	**34**	11	1	9	**45**	4
9	0	16	**28**	15	1	**28**	14	16
10	9	**35**	12	4	12	**26**	20	2
11	1	15	19	**24**	0	**28**	7	25
12	1	15	**37**	7	0	5	**45**	10
13	2	20	**29**	8	1	8	**47**	4
14	2	18	**23**	17	6	11	**39**	4
15	0	22	**28**	10	0	6	**49**	5
16	1	21	**32**	6	1	10	**46**	3
17	4	18	**27**	11	5	13	**35**	7
18	5	12	18	**24**	3	14	18	**25**
19	1	11	18	**30**	3	7	15	**35**
20	1	15	**31**	13	0	13	**27**	20
21	2	13	**31**	14	0	16	**26**	18
22	2	23	7	**28**	5	11	16	**28**
23	0	18	**31**	11	0	**30**	16	13
24	3	18	15	**24**	3	16	12	**29**
25	2	11	14	**33**	2	9	11	**28**
26	4	5	11	**40**	4	2	4	**50**
27	1	12	15	**31**	1	4	4	**51**
28	0	4	24	**32**	0	1	12	**47**

Note. In each condition the white and black students' responses have been combined. A description of each item is found in Table 14. In rare cases an item did not get recorded; this is why some of the frequencies sum to 59. In each condition the modal frequency is set in boldface. Items 9, 11, and 23 show the modals for different stages indicating one of the differences produced by the conditions. The tendency for items that share the same modal category to have a higher modal frequency in condition C is seen in this table.

believes all items e, f, and g and fully rejects all items h, i, and j. (Notice again that the person can still believe many things other than e, f, and g.)

Consider another person (or the same person seen at a much later time) who is said to be in a later stage y. We say that a person is said to be in the later stage provided that he fully endorses items h, i, and j and fully rejects items e, f, and g. In terms of the sorting task, such a definition of stages would require that all experimental subjects invariably place items e, f, and g together in the first cluster and never place either h, i, or j in the first cluster but invariably place them together in a separate cluster.

In terms of the modal response concept, this delineation of stages would require that 100 percent of the subjects place a particular item into one stage only. Item f, for example, would have all frequencies in a single stage and would have a frequency of zero for every other stage. Some other items may not be indicative of any particular stage, and these items might very well show an even distribution of frequencies in every stage. With respect to our present results (see Table 14 and Table 18), items 1 through 7 seem to come closest to satisfying the definition just supplied; but because not all items have the pattern of item, we must reject this particular definition of stages.

A second possibility in defining the idea of a stage is as follows. Suppose that a person can really be said to be in some particular stage x (at a particular point in time) but that one can *never point to any critically defining attributes* that will unambiguously guarantee the existence of the cognitive stage. In this sense, the attributes or beliefs that a person in stage x will endorse are only probabilistically determined. (That is, all the items will tend to have some positive entry for each stage, and no stage will attract all the frequencies.) Our data, by and large, seem to fit this conception quite nicely. What is needed in order to account for the additional aspect of our data that we have called the generalization gradient is to suppose that one can depict the stages as ideal points in some dimensional space and represent the test items as points in this space. With this dimensional representation, one can account for both the probabilistic features of the data and the magnitudes for each of the probabilistic entries. It would take us too far afield to test this idea in full detail here, because it would involve developing precise mathematical statements of the assumptions of the model. We do hope to present this conception elsewhere, however.

There is yet a third type of model that can be distinguished. Here the notion of stage is regarded as merely a convenient label attached to a cluster of beliefs that tend to occur together in time and very gradually merge into another set of beliefs at some later point in time. We believe the notion fails to account for the persistent regularities in people's judgments about which items belong together.

Conclusions

There are two major shortcomings to the study under discussion. First, the research dealt with verbalizations and not directly with the way people feel—yet the identity stages themselves are intensely personal experiences. Second, black college students in general and black college students in highly selective institutions are not typical of American black people. We consider it a reasonable assumption, however, that verbal statements are related to the way people feel and that black college students, even at selective institutions, have experienced some of the same aspects of black living as have other black people. It is a worn joke that researchers in psychology use a small segment of the population (e.g., college sophomores) and generalize about all people when studying human traits and relationships, so that we must indeed be cautious. Thus, even though the stages in black identity hypothesized by Cross were confirmed in our study of black college students at a particular institution, results should be replicated with a sample more representative of the black population before the stages are confirmed in a definitive way.

Cross's hypothesis concerning the existence of several stages in the development of black awareness in the United States has received general positive support in the Hall-Freedle-Cross study. However, some details of the hypothesis, such as which particular items are indicative of particular stages, were found to need modification. In addition, the imprecise statement of some items may lead to ambiguous readings and for this reason need to be restated or elaborated in greater detail.

The existence of a generalization gradient was argued to provide support for the position suggested originally by Cross that the four underlying stages occur in a definite order—i.e., pre-encounter, encounter, immersion, and internalization.

There is a pronounced tendency for white students to perceive these stages and the items that characterize them in much the same manner that black students perceive them. However, a few significant differences between blacks and whites in response to particular items were noted.

There was an impressive similarity in sorting patterns across experimental conditions (conditions B and C), which argues for the general strength of the underlying conception—i.e., that the results are fairly replicable under rather differing testing conditions. And a generalization gradient can still be found even for condition C (which provided the subjects with semantic labels for and descriptions of each stage); this fact argues for the nontriviality of the sorting task. That is, had this condition resulted in the unique placement of every item into precisely one stage (with 100 percent agreement among subjects as to which stage each item belonged in), the researchers would have then been open to the criticism that the task given the subjects was simply to match items to categories where both the items and the categories to which they belonged were simply part of the common knowledge of the population. The fact that this did not occur either within or across conditions argues for the meaningfulness of the judgments made in the experiment.

Some Linguistic Consequences of the Study

Hall, Freedle, and Cross (1972) have documented stages in the evolution of black self-identity. These stages involve shifts in cognitive functions that have impact on self-evaluation and goal-directedness. By implication, these large-scale shifts must enter into language functioning. Language is merely one part of the whole human being. We would predict that language functioning must change as a consequence of self-identity changes. In particular, those language registers, which in the early stages were reserved for demonstrating deference across minority-majority lines (e.g., shucking), should drop out of the language repertoire of blacks as they move through the stages articulated by Hall, Freedle, and Cross. In like manner, new registers appropriate to the semantic content of the later stages should emerge.

OTHER STUDIES ON SELF-CONCEPT

The research on the self-concept of young children is varied. Some of it supports older findings that focused on the "disadvantaged" aspects of black life, while other research examines the impact of the black movement of the 1960s.

Early work by Clark and Clark (1939, 1940) is continually referred to. In this work, the Clarks investigated the aspect of race consciousness as related to the development of self-consciousness in young black children. They found that when given a choice between identifying themselves with line drawings of a white boy, a black boy, or animals, the group of subjects (150 black children in segregated nursery schools) chose the black boy more often than the white boy. As age increased, their choices of the black boy increased, and those of the animals decreased. The Clarks' 1940 study further investigated race consciousness along these lines, concentrating, however, more specifically on the factor of skin color and its influence on racial identification and awareness. Using the same subjects, they subdivided the children according to gradations into light, medium, or dark. The same line drawings were used, omitting the animal choice. Here the results showed that as one moved from the light to the darker groups, the choice of the black boy over the white boy increased. That is, the light subjects identified more with the white boy, and the medium and dark subjects identified more with the black boy. The Clarks concluded that an important factor in the development of consciousness of self and racial identification is skin color, and also that identification of one's own race is made on the basis of physical characteristics rather than socially defined characteristics of racial groups.

Greenwald and Oppenheim (1968) replicated the studies of Clark and Clark (1939, 1940) with some changes in experimental procedure. They found that by adding a doll of intermediate color to the white and dark brown dolls the greater misidentification of black children decreased. In fact, the percentage was about the same as misidentification by white children of the same age. The investigators did find, however, that the children's evaluative responses to the dolls revealed the greater unpopularity of the black dolls.

This is an interesting finding because it suggests that many of the children tend to persist in responding in a way that can be interpreted as reflecting stage 1 notions of self as set forth by Hall, Freedle, and Cross. We may be dealing here with a cultural lag phenomenon, i.e., the actual socialization of children in a culture may change very slowly in spite of a radical reassessment of one's self-image as an adult. If this is so, one would predict that in ten or twenty years one might see measurable changes in the way blacks rear their children. This could include the abandonment of positional control uses of language in favor of the more personal modes, which might eventually result in children having a more positive evaluation of self.

Morland (1966) compared young black children from a northern community with integrated schools with those from a southern community with segregated schools. He found that in both regions, white subjects identified with and preferred members of their own race, while black subjects also identified with and preferred whites.

Williams (1969) compared the self-concept of black preschool children in integrated suburban community programs with children in segregated urban community programs. He also looked at the effect on self-concept of the presence or absence of the father. His data showed that the boys from the suburban and urban programs did not differ in self-concept, but the girls in the suburban programs had higher self-concepts than those in the urban program. There were no differences in the self-concepts of boys and girls from father-absent homes in the urban community, suggesting that the absence of a father is not as important to the development of the black boy as it is to the development of the white boy. This particular finding is not surprising, given our early review of ethnocentrism in social science research.

McAdoo (1971) investigated the relationship between the self-concept of black preschool children and their evaluative attitudes toward whites and blacks. She found no significant correlation between the two, but she did find that the children in her northern and southern samples differed on self-concept. The children in the southern, rural, all-black community had significantly higher self-concepts than did those from the northern, urban, integrated community. These groups did not differ on racial attitudes. Also, children from broken homes scored higher on all self-concept measures than did those from homes that were intact.

This is an especially important finding. The so-called separate but equal system of the South allowed one to know exactly where he stood in the system at large—indeed there was no ambiguity. One could, with few financial resources, achieve status and relative affluence through the network of higher educational opportunities provided by the traditional black colleges and the separate and discriminatory employment system. It follows from such a system that there is less confusion about who one is because one's role in the system is quite clearly defined. On the other hand, in the northern urban community, equality is often more ideal than real—thereby creating ambiguity about who one is, what one can achieve, and what process to employ for such a quest.

A further association one might offer to the McAdoo study concerns the hypothesis relating self-esteem and language usage. We noted earlier that Coppinger and Ammons (1952) found an increasing discrepancy in IQ scores between rural and urban groups after the age of 9. This result, placed in line with McAdoo's (1971) rural-urban difference in self-esteem, invites a simplistic interlinking of these results. Such an argument would go as follows:

1. IQ scores implicate language proficiency.
2. A high IQ score suggests high language competence.
3. This finding obtains for urban subjects.
4. Blacks in the urban North score lower in self-esteem than do those in the rural South.
5. The fallacious conclusion would be that low self-esteem is correlated with higher intelligence.

Fortunately Burke (1969) found that such relationships do not obtain. In particular, he found no significant correlations between the intelligence scores and creativity or self-concept measures for black third graders in a de facto segregated school. Indeed, the place to look for positive relationships between self-esteem and language usage may not be in the tangled area of IQ test scores, but in an ethnographic usage of different language registers as a function of the individual's self-esteem.

THE RELATIONSHIP BETWEEN SELF-CONCEPT AND SOCIAL COMMUNICATION: A HYPOTHESIS

We wish to forestall simple cause-effect linkages between self-concept and the affective content of social communication. Individuals are not static entities. They have the potential for change over time. As a substitute for simple cause-effect models and to stimulate a more subtle approach to the problem we shall outline a flow model which captures the complex interlinkages between self-concept and social communication. This model will then lead us to an outline of future work.

Figure 4 sketches some ways in which the social communication styles of blacks interacting with either blacks or whites is affected by self-concept and by changes which, in turn, lead to changes in the self-concept.

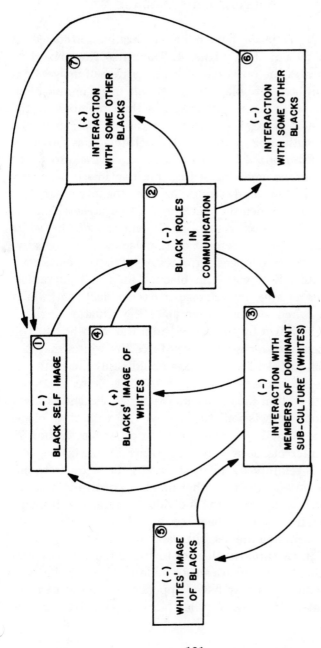

FIGURE 4

A flow model showing changes in stage of the black person's self-concept
(self-image) as it relates to social communication affect.

Initially the black person has a negative self-image, as designated by box 1 in Figure 4. The arrow from box 1 to box 2 indicates the outcome of his negative self-image: he is prepared, in box 2, to play a negative role in communication. In box 3, when he is interacting with a member of the dominant subculture, the effect is negative. This leads to a further strengthening of the negative self-image, as shown by the arrow from box 3 back to box 1. The figure also shows the black person emerging with a positive image of whites (see box 4). Repeated swings around the cycle serve to maintain or strengthen the black person's negative self-image. The arrow from box 3 to box 5 emphasizes the white person's further reinforcement of the black person's negative self-image, which happens as a result of a white person's negative interaction with the black. This result guarantees that further negative interchanges between blacks and whites will occur when another communication situation presents itself; this is shown by the arrow from box 5 to box 3. This subcycle serves to maintain or reinforce the whites' negative image of blacks. Additional boxes could easily illustrate that the white adopts a positive self-image as a result of his negative interaction with a black. The figure also shows that a black person interacts sometimes negatively with other blacks (box 6) and sometimes positively with other blacks (box 7). When he interacts negatively with other blacks his negative self-image is reinforced; this is shown by the arrow from box 6 back to box 1. On the other hand, a positive interaction with other blacks lessens the individual's negative self-image. The arrow from box 7 back to box 1 thus indicates the potential of altering the negative value of box 1.

Now let us suppose that historical circumstances have allowed the black American to redefine himself in more positive terms. This may have happened as a result of many positive interactions with other blacks that led to creative insight into how the condition of all blacks might be bettered. While it is difficult to document, one might also suppose that numerous interactions of the following subcycle have occurred: 1 to 2 to 7 back to 1 with many repetitions that will lead to a positive self-image. In turn, the negative value in box 2 could gradually become positive. This should lead to fewer negative interactions with other blacks. In effect, this would lead to a disruption or attenuation of the following subcycle: 1 to 2 to 6 back to 1. Similarly, as blacks increase their positive self-image, they are prepared to play more positive roles in communicating with people, be they white or black. Because of this the value in box 3, representing interaction with members of the dominant subculture, will tend to become more positive, which in turn will lead to further reinforcment of a positive black self-image. Hence, the arrow leading from box 3 back to box 1 will become positive and will reinforce or maintain a positive black self-image.

Blacks' images of whites that result from positive interaction will also reinforce the blacks' positive images of whites. This occurs in box 4.

A dynamic model gives us some insight into the complexities that must be considered in articulating a more complete information-processing model, one that illustrates the manner in which such cognitive notions as self-concept can interact with language-communication style. Further specifications of the model could articulate the effects of formal versus informal situations, of dialect spoken, of particular topics, and of other sociolinguistic variables. In addition, a fuller model would introduce more precise quantitative functions that would reflect the changes in internal cognitive structure and external speech. These serve as a function of successive enounters with other members of the embedded subculture as compared with interactions with members of the dominant culture. We have yet to do this. We shall now describe some future studies that will provide us with a data base from which a more complete model can be constructed.

FUTURE STUDIES

More ethnographic investigations to determine naturalistic modes of language usage can be done. We have described how subcultural experiences can lead to different principles of language usage and cognitive functioning. In all the descriptions, extensive data are needed of a more immediate nature, that is, direct observation of several age groups of black and white children of different socioeconomic backgrounds and in several naturally occurring settings such as school classrooms, school playgrounds, home settings with just the immediate family present, and home settings with outside visitors of varying age groups present.

The language patterns (language registers) evoked by the different naturalistic settings can be studied in conjunction with more controlled experimental settings of such types as sentence imitation, story recall, story production (given a topic), and sentence comprehension.

In designing each such controlled study, one should select materials that allow study of the contributory effects of memory, perception, and problem solving in language usage. Given these measurable effects, one can then attempt to use the scores to interpret the patterns that emerge from the naturalistic settings.)

A third group of studies could assign rather open-ended tasks (verbal and nonverbal) to groups of children to examine how the tasks alter their interaction.

Further groupings of select populations from both urban and rural areas (black and white; middle and low socioeconomic level) could be tried with the number of children present varied. Small numbers may facilitate cooperative interaction while large numbers may induce segregation and suspicion among the children.

And finally, groups of adults could be studied along similar lines.

CONCLUSION

Cognitive assessment across cultures typically has involved comparison of many cultures that are relatively separate and independent geographically and politically. Anyone trying to assess the cultural patterns and abilities of members of embedded subcultures (for example, blacks) in the United States, however, must add a level of analysis to the usual pattern. This is because the embedded subculture by definition is one that must function as though it were an integral part of the larger culture but with few of the rights and privileges of that larger culture; the status of its members is subordinate to that of members of the majority. The need for an additional level of analysis was a major theme of this book.

The second major theme was an examination of the feedback mechanisms that maintain the relative status of one subgroup with respect to other subgroups. These feedback loops were postulated to operate at individual as well as institutional levels of the majority culture and the minority subcultures.

Individuals do not exist in a societal vacuum. Rather, they interrelate with individuals who share their own cultural tradition, and they also interact with individuals from different cultural traditions. In western industrialized nations, a full appreciation of cultural tensions had led us to the important concept of subcultural embedding within a majority culture. The particular qualities of this subcultural experience leave their imprint on the individual's patterns of behavior at many levels; some of these are language usage (dialect), self-identity, problem-solving ability, and intellectual functioning. We have attempted to document the idea that general cognitive functioning is affected by the socio-economic pressures particular to the subcultural experience. These pressures are especially damaging when the subculture resides in a majority culture that has a history of racism.

The irony of a racist position is that no clear referent is scientifically justifiable as the target of racial oppression. Physical anthropologists have been unable to agree on an adequate classification system for race. Consequently, they are unable to state the number of races that exist. The uncertainty of these schemata stems from the impossibility of drawing arbitrary lines of demarcation on essentially continuous distributions of physical traits. Thus on the feature of skin color, for example, it has been impossible to justify any one point of demarcation that leads to a classification of light skin versus dark skin. Yet in the everyday operation of cultures and subcultures clear racial classification is assumed to exist. Even in social scientific circles the myth of clear racial classifications has emerged in the form of genetic hypotheses concerning race and behavior. The subtlety of cultural difference has eluded many of these scientists.

We have summarized the ethnocentric stance of some social scientists, which also stems from a failure to appreciate cultural subtleties. In particular, Moynihan's characterization of the black family as pathological was criticized as reflecting an ethnocentric stance. In this case, Moynihan takes as the norm middle-class customs and behaviors; hence, in his view deviations from this norm must be pathological. The deficiency of this viewpoint is self-evident. Yet old myths such as this die slowly. One reason is that such myths become self-perpetuating through feedback loops in the majority and minority cultures. Even in higher scientific circles, the cultural background of individual scientists may cloud their reasoning when it is necessary to evaluate subcultural patterns. A way out of this dilemma can be found in starting with the assumption of *cultural pluralism*. One who started with this viewpoint might incorporate the major themes from minority life as well as those from mainstream culture, ascribing equal validity to each when assessing behavioral patterns of groups. A methodology for gaining a clear understanding of subcultural embedding in terms of what it is, how it functions, and how it maintains these functions through time would come from an ethnographic examination of behaviors in their naturalistic settings.

A good part of this book has focused on the black American experience. In particular, the language of black Americans has been examined as a major reflection of subcultural embeddedness. It has been our thesis that one can not understand the structure and function of black language without relating it to the larger social sphere. Available data suggest that the conditions under which one learns a language system such as standard English (SE) and its variants, for example, black English vernacular (BEV), influence the way the two systems are organized in memory. When they are learned in a unicultural environment where they function somewhat interchangeably, they appear to be organized as a single cognitive system. Later in life, when persons who use the dual system become exposed increasingly to communities other than their own, whose language functions and rules are noticeably different, they appear to cognitively separate standard English and black English vernacular into distinct systems which have only partial interconnections. The effect of the environment appears to be responsible for this cognitive restructuring.

Exposure to the school system is often a negative experience for minority individuals since it can set up conditions for numerous negative feedback loops to operate. Piestrup (1973) found, in her study of teaching styles and school learning, that of six such styles the one that incorporated the black American life-style and language system into the first grade curriculum had the greatest impact on reading performance. This may be described as a positive feedback loop which employs the natural features of the subcultural experience so as to move, in this case, school-children to higher levels of cognitive achievement. Moreover, Piestrup found that some of the other five teaching styles created negative feedback loops that interfered with the children's reaching higher levels of cognitive achievement.

An analysis of intraindividual language functions across members of subcultures revealed strong preferences for one dialect over another, depending on the class and "race" the person belonged to. Membership in any of the four sub-cultures (lower-class blacks, middle-class blacks, lower-class whites, and middle-class whites) did not affect the measured ability to store and retrieve sentences from memory. What did affect it was dialect preference. This task suggested that the notion of subculture and dialect are important considera-tions in interpreting such experimental results. An additional outcome of this study suggested that a greater cognitive load was borne by blacks than by whites. This was traceable to the greater frequency with which blacks translated from one dialect into another. The whites tended to employ only a single dialect and therefore carried out fewer translations than did the blacks; this meant they had fewer cognitive operations to perform and hence carried a lighter cognitive load.

Additional demonstration of our two major themes comes from a consideration of the assessment of intellectual functioning and problem solving.

During the last ten years a major point of view regarding intellectual functioning is that expressed by Jensen (1969), who argues that blacks are genetically inferior to whites. A careful examination of the available data found Jensen's interpretation to be quite insensitive to the power of culture in molding and directing its members to utilize and develop their mental resources. Other work dealing with intellectual functioning and problem solving was examined. We found that many of these studies not only were ponderously conceived but also were executed in such a way as to call into question their interpretation.

Finally, this book argued for a relationship between black language and black self-identity, i.e., that the social milieu of oppression must influence one's self-concept and that the self-concept which evolves must affect the manner in which such individuals communicate within their own subculture and across subcultures. Such a view represents our synthesizing attempt to view the individual as a totality. This is somewhat counter to the analytic tendency in some quarters of social science.

As shown by the data on black Americans identity formation, the movement has been through four stages, from pre-encounter to encounter to immersion to internalization. A model was presented that argued for a close connection between the affective content of communicative encounters and the dynamic effect this has on the individual's subsequent encounters. A nonlinear system of feedback loops was found to be useful in constructing this model. But much work remains to be done in detailing, through empirical and naturalistic study, the full complexity of how language, self-concept, cognition, and subcultural embedding interact in producing an organized view of the individual.

More importantly, the fleshing out of such a model can lead to a greater understanding of those salient cultural institutions, e.g., the schools, that will make effective use of existing subcultural behaviors so as to make the melting pot a reality, not a myth, through cultural pluralism.

BIBLIOGRAPHY

Alland, A.
Human diversity. Garden City, N.Y.: Anchor Press-Doubleday, 1973.

Anastasi, A.
Heredity, environment, and the question, how? *Psychological Review*, 1958, **65**, 197-208.

Anastasi, A.
Culture fair testing. *Education Digest*, 1965, **30**, 9-11.

Baratz, J. C.
A bidialectal task for determining language proficiency in economically disadvantaged children. *Child Development*, 1969, **40**(3), 889-901.

Baratz, J. C.
Language abilities of black Americans: Review of research. Unpublished manuscript, 1971.

Baratz, J. C., & Baratz, S.
Early childhood intervention: The social science base of institutional racism. *Harvard Educational Review*, 1970, **40**, 1-22.

Bee, H. L., Van Egeren, L. F., Streissguth, A. P., Nyman, B. A., & Leckie, M. S.
Social class differences in maternal teaching strategies and

speech patterns. *Developmental Psychology*, 1969, **1**, 726-734.

Bernstein, B.

Class, codes and control (Vol. 1). *Theoretical studies towards a sociology of language.* London: Routledge & Kegan Paul, 1971. (Reissued 1974.)

Blank, M., & Solomon, F.

A tutorial language program to develop abstract thinking in socially disadvantaged preschool children. *Child Development*, 1968, **39**(2), 379-389.

Boas, F.

Some traits of primitive culture. *Journal of American Folklore*, 1905, **17**, 243-254.

Boas, F.

The mind of primitive man. New York: The Free Press, 1965. (Originally published, 1911.)

Burke, B. P.

An exploratory study of the relationships among third grade Negro children's self-concept, creativity and intelligence, and teachers' perceptions of those relationships. *Dissertation Abstracts International*, 1969, **30**, 4A, 1327-1328.

Burt, C.

The evidence for the concept of intelligence. *British Journal of Educational Psychology*, 1955, **25**, 158-177.

Burt, C.

The distribution of intelligence. *British Journal of Psychology*, 1957, **48**, 161-175.

Burt, C.

The inheritance of mental ability. *American Psychology*, 1958, **13**, 1-15.

Burt, C.

Class difference in general intelligence: III. *British Journal of Statistical Psychology*, 1959, **12**, 15-33.

Burt, C.

Intelligence and social mobility. *British Journal of Statistical Psychology*, 1961, 14, 3–24.

Burt, C.

Is intelligence distributed normally? *British Journal of Statistical Psychology*, 1963, 16, 175–190.

Burt, C.

The genetic determination of differences in intelligence: A study of monozygotic twins reared together and apart. *British Journal of Psychology*, 1966, 57, 137–153.

Burt, C.

Mental capacity and its critics. *Bulletin of the British Psychological Society*, 1968, 21, 11–18.

Burt, C., & Howard, M.

The multifactorial theory of inheritance and its application to intelligence. *British Journal of Statistical Psychology*, 1956, 9, 95–131.

Burt, C., & Howard, M.

The relative influence of heredity and environment of assessments of intelligence. *British Journal of Statistical Psychology*, 1957, 10, 99–104.

Carroll, J. B., & Casagrande, J. B.

The function of language classification on behavior. In E. E. Maccoby, T. M. Newcomb, & E. L. Hartley (Eds.), *Readings in social psychology* (3rd ed.). New York: Holt, Rinehart & Winston, 1958.

Cazden, C.

Child language and interaction. New York: Holt, Rinehart & Winston, 1972.

Cazden, C., John-Steiner, V. P., & Hymes, D.

Functions of language in the classroom. New York: Columbia University, Teachers College Press, 1972.

Chomsky, N.

Language and mind. New York: Harcourt Brace Jovanovich, 1968.

Clark, K. B., & Clark, M. K.
Segregation as a factor in the racial identification of Negro preschool children. *Journal of Experimental Education*, 1939, 8, 161–163.

Clark, K. B., & Clark, M. K.
Skin color as a factor in racial identification of Negro preschool children. *Journal of Social Psychology*, 1940, 11, 159–169.

Cole, M., Gay, J., Glick, J. A., & Sharp, D. W.
The cultural context of learning and thinking. New York: Basic Books, 1971.

Cole, M., & Scribner, S.
Culture and thought: A psychological introduction. New York: John Wiley & Sons, 1974.

Cook-Gumperz, J.
Social control and socialization: A study of class differences in the language of maternal control. London: Routledge, Kegan & Paul, 1973.

Coppinger, N. E., & Ammons, R. B.
The full-range picture vocabulary test: VIII. A normative study of Negro children. *Journal of Clinical Psychology*, 1952, 8, 136–140.

Cronbach, L.
Heredity, environment and educational policy. *Harvard Educational Review*, 1969, 39, 338–347.

Cross, W.
The black experience viewed as a process; A crude model for black self-actualization. Paper presented at the 34th annual meeting of the Association of Social and Behavioral Scientists, Tallahassee, Fla., April 1970.

Crow, J. F.
Genetic theories and influences: Comments on the value of diversity. *Harvard Educational Review*, 1969, 39, 301–309.

Dawis, R. V., Soriano, L. V., Siojo, L. R., & Haynes, J.
Demographic factors in the education of relations in analogy word pairs (Tech. Rep. 3). Minneapolis: University of Minnesota, Department of Psychology, 1974.

Downs, J. S.
Cultures in crisis. Beverly Hills, Calif.: Glencoe Press, 1971.

Downs, J. S., & Bleibtreu, H.
Human variation. Beverly Hills, Calif.: Glencoe Press, 1969.

Ferguson, C. A.
Language problems of variation and repetoire. *Daedalus*, 1973, **102**(3), 37–46.

Frake, C. O.
Notes on queries in ethnography. *The American Anthropologist*, 1964, **66**(3), 132–145.

Freedle, R. O., & Hall, W. S.
An information-processing approach to some problems in developmental sociolinguistics. Paper presented at the biennial meeting of the International Society for the Study of Behavioral Development, Ann Arbor: University of Michigan, August 1973.

Garvey, G., & McFarlane, P.
A measure of standard English proficiency of inner-city children. *American Educational Research Journal*, 1970, **7**, 29–40.

Geertz, C.
Impact of the concept of culture on the concept of man. In E. Hammel & W. Simmons (Eds.), *Man makes sense.* Boston: Little, Brown and Co., 1970.

Glazer, N., & Moynihan, D. P.
Beyond the melting pot: The Negroes, Puerto Ricans, Jews, Italians, and Irish of New York City. Cambridge, Mass.: MIT Press, 1963.

Gottesman, I.
Biogenetics of race and class. In M. Deutsch, I. Katz, & A. Jensen (Eds.), *Social class, race and psychological development*. New York: Holt, Rinehart & Winston, 1968.

Gray, S. W., & Klaus, R. A.
An experimental preschool program for culturally deprived children. *Child Development*, 1965, 36(4), 887–898.

Greenwald, H. J., & Oppenheim, D. B.
Reported magnitude of self-misidentification among Negro children: Artifact. *Journal of Personality and Social Psychology*, 1968, 8(1), 49–52.

Hall, W. S., & Freedle, R.
A developmental investigation of standard and nonstandard English among black and white children. *Human Development*, 1973, 16(6), 440–464.

Hall, W. S., Freedle, R., & Cross, W. E.
Stages in the development of a black identity (Research Report No. 50). Iowa City, Iowa: American College Testing Program, April 1972.

Halliday, M.
Explorations in the functions of language. London: Edward Arnold Publishers, 1973.

Harris, M.
The rise of anthropological theory. New York: Crowell, 1968.

Heider, E. R., Cazden, C. B., & Brown, R.
Social class differences in the effectiveness style of children's coding ability (Project Literacy Report No. 9). Ithaca, N.Y.: Cornell University, 1968. Mimeographed.

Herskovits, M. J.
The myth of the Negro past. Boston: Beacon Press, 1941.

Herskovits, M. J.
Preface. In F. Boas, *The mind of primitive man*. New York: The Free Press, 1965.

Hill, R.
Strengths of black families. New York: Emerson Hall, 1972.

Hockett, C.
Chinese versus English: An exploration of the Whorfian thesis. In H. Hoijer (Ed.), *Language in culture*, Chicago: University of Chicago Press, 1954.

Hollingshead, A. B., & Redlich, F. C.
Social class and mental illness: A community study. New York: John Wiley & Sons, 1958.

Horner, V. M.
The verbal world of the lower class three year old; A pilot study in linguistic ecology. Unpublished doctoral dissertation, University of Rochester, 1968.

Hunt, J. McV.
Has compensatory education failed? Has it been attempted? *Harvard Educational Review*, 1969, **39**(2), 278–300.

Hymes, D.
On the origins and foundations of inequality among speakers. *Daedalus*, 1973, 59–86.

Jencks, C.
Inequality: A reassessment of the effect of family and schooling in America. New York: Basic Books, 1972.

Jensen, A. R.
How much can we boost IQ and scholastic achievement? *Harvard Educational Review*, 1969, **39**, 1–123.

Jones, J.
Prejudice and racism. Reading, Mass.: Addison-Wesley, 1972.

Kagan, J. S.
Inadequate evidence and illogical conclusions. *Harvard Educational Review*, 1969, **39**, 274–277.

Kendler, T. S., Kendler, H. H., & Carrick, M. A.
The effect of verbal labels and inferential problem solution. *Child Development*, 1966, **40**, 749–763.

Krauss, R. M., & Glucksberg, S.
The development of communication: Competence as a function of age. *Child Development*, 1967, **40**, 255-260.

Kroeber, A. L.
Anthropology: Race, language, culture, psychology, prehistory. New York: Harcourt Brace Jovanovich, 1948.

Kuhn, T.
The structure of scientific revolutions. Chicago: University of Chicago Press, 1970.

Labov, W.
The logic of non-standard English. In F. Williams (Ed.), *Language and poverty.* Chicago: Markham, 1970.

Leacock, E. B.
Distortions of working-class reality in American social science. *Science and Society,* 1967, **31**, 1-21.

Leacock, E. B.
Introduction. In E. B. Leacock (Ed.), *The culture of poverty: A critique.* New York: Simon & Schuster, 1971.

Levine, R. A.
Cross-cultural study in child psychology. In P. H. Mussen (Ed.), *Carmichael's manual of child psychology* (Vol. 2). 1970.

Luria, A. R.
Towards the problem of the historical nature of psychological processes. *International Journal of Psychology,* 1971, **6**, 259-272.

McAdoo, H. A.
Racial attitudes and self-concepts of black preschool children. *Dissertation Abstracts International,* 1971, **31**, 8A, 3963.

McDermott, R.
Achieving school failure: An anthropological approach to illiteracy and social stratification. In G. Spindler (Ed.),

Education and cultural process. New York: Holt, Rinehart & Winston, 1974.

McDermott, R.
The cultural context of learning to read. In S. Wanat, H. Singer, & M. Kling (Eds.), *Extracting meaning from written language.* Newark, Del.: International Reading Association, 1975.

Melamed, P. A.
Black English phonology: The question of reading interference. *Monographs of the Language-Behavior Research Laboratory*, Berkeley: University of California, Language-Behavior Research Laboratory, 1971, No. 1.

Montagu, A.
The concept of race. New York: The Free Press, 1964.

Montagu, A.
Man's most dangerous myth: The fallacy of race. Cleveland: World Publishing Company, 1965.

Morland, J. K.
A comparison of race awareness in northern and southern children. *American Journal of Orthopsychiatry*, 1966, 36(1), 22–31.

Moynihan, D. P.
The Negro family. Washington, D.C.: U.S. Department of Labor, Office of Policy Planning and Research, 1965.

Newman, H. H., Freeman, F. N., & Holzinger, K. J.
Twins: A study of heredity and environment. Chicago: University of Chicago Press, 1937.

Osterberg, R.
Bilingualism and the first school language. Umea, Sweden: Vastenbottens Togeker, A,B, 1961.

Piaget, J.
Necessité et signification des rechèrches comparatives en psychologie génétique. *International Journal of Psychology*, 1966, 1, 3–13.

Piestrup, A. McC.
Black dialect interference and accommodation of reading instruction in first grade. *Monographs of the Language-Behavior Research Laboratory*, Berkeley: University of California, Language-Behavior Research Laboratory, 1973, No. 4.

Quay, L. C.
Language, dialect, reinforcement, and the intelligence test performance of Negro children. *Child Development*, 1971, 42, 5–15.

Quay, L. C.
Negro dialect and Binet performance in severely disadvantaged black four year olds. *Child Development*, 1972, 43, 245–250.

Quay, L. C.
Language dialect, age, and intelligence test performance in disadvantaged black children. *Child Development*, 1974, 45, 463–468.

Rentel, V., & Kennedy, J.
Effects of pattern drill on the phonology, syntax and reading achievement of rural Appalachian children. *American Educational Research Journal*, 1972, 9, 87–100.

Rist, R.
The urban school; A factory of failure. Cambridge, Mass.: MIT Press, 1973.

Ruddell, R. B.
An investigation of the effect of the similarity of oral and written patterns of language structure on reading comprehension. Unpublished doctoral dissertation, Indiana University, 1963.

Rystrom, R.
Dialect training and reading: A further look. *Reading Research Quarterly*, 1970, 5, 581–589.

Shockley, W.
Dysgenics, geneticity, raceology: A challenge to the intellectual responsibility of educators. *Phi Delta Kappan*, 1972, 300.

Shuey, A.
The testing of Negro intelligence (2nd ed.). New York: Social Science Press, 1966.

Shuy, R.
The concept of gradatum in language learning. Paper presented at the American Sociological Association Meeting, Montreal, 1973.

Simons, H. D.
Black dialect and reading interference: A review and analysis of the research evidence. Berkeley: University of California, School of Education, 1973. Mimeographed.

Sims, R.
A psycholinguistic description of miscues created by selected young readers during oral reading of text in black dialect and standard English. Unpublished doctoral dissertation, Wayne State University, 1972.

Stewart, W. A.
On the use of Negro dialect in the teaching of reading. In J. C. Baratz & R. Shuy (Eds.), *Teaching black children to read.* Washington, D.C.: Center for Applied Linguistics, 1969.

Tatham, S. M.
Reading comprehension of materials written with select oral language patterns: A study at grades two and four. *Reading Research Quarterly*, 1970, 5, 402–426.

Terry, R.
For whites only. Grand Rapids, Mich.: Eerdmans, 1970.

Turner, L.
Africanism in the Gullah dialect. Chicago: University of Chicago Press, 1949.

Valentine, C. A.
   Culture and poverty: Critique and counter proposals.
   Chicago: University of Chicago Press, 1968.
Valentine, C. A.
   The culture of poverty: Its scientific significance and its
   implications for action. In E. B. Leacock (Ed.), *The
   culture of poverty: A critique.* New York: Simon &
   Schuster, 1971.
Vygotsky, L. S.
   Thought and language. Cambridge, Mass.: MIT Press,
   1962. English translation.
Ward, M. C.
   Them children: A study in language learning. New York:
   Holt, Rinehart & Winston, 1971.
Whorf, B. L.
   Language, thought and reality. Boston: MIT Press; New
   York: John Wiley & Sons, 1956.
Williams, D. E.
   Self-concept and verbal mental ability in Negro preschool
   children. *Dissertation Abstracts*, 1969, 29, 9B, 3475.
Williams, F., & Naremore, A. C.
   Social class differences in children's syntactic per-
   formance. *Journal of Speech and Hearing Research*,
   1969, 12, 778–793.
Williams, R., & Rivers, W.
   Mismatches in testing from black English. Paper read at
   the annual meeting of the American Psychological Associ-
   ation, Honolulu, 1972.
Young, V. H.
   Family and childhood in a southern Negro community.
   American Anthropologist, 1970, 72(2), 269–288.
Young, V. H.
   A black American socialization pattern. *American Ethno-
   logist*, 1974, 1(2), 405–412.

INDEX

Numbers in italics refer to the pages on which the complete references are cited.